∞

And the Word
Dwelt Among Us

Other books
by Romano Guardini
available from Sophia Institute Press:

Eternal Life
The Art of Praying
The Rosary of Our Lady
Learning the Virtues That Lead You to God
Preparing Yourself for Mass
The Lord's Prayer
The Living God

Romano Guardini

And the
Word
Dwelt Among Us

Meeting the Living God in Scripture

SOPHIA INSTITUTE PRESS®
Manchester, New Hampshire

And the Word Dwelt Among Us: Meeting the Living God in Scripture was first published in Würzburg in 1949 and in 1958 by Werkbund-Verlag under the title *Drei Schriftauslegungen*. In 1993, Matthias-Grünewald-Verlag published a pocketbook edition under the title *Geistliche Schriftauslegung*. In 1963, Henry Regnery Company published an English translation by Stella Lange entitled *The Word of God: On Faith, Hope and Charity*. This 1998 edition by Sophia Institute Press uses Regnery's 1963 translation, with minor editorial revisions throughout the text.

Printed in the United States of America

Jacket design by Lorraine Bilodeau

The cover artwork is a detail of Albrecht Dürer's
Self-Portrait with Fur Coat at Age 28, Alte Pinakothek,
Munich, Germany (Scala/Art Resource, New York).

Sophia Institute Press®
Box 5284, Manchester, NH 03108
1-800-888-9344

Nihil Obstat: Rev. George J. O'Kelly, S.J., *Censor*
Imprimatur: Rt. Rev. Msgr. George J. Casey, *Vicar General*

Library of Congress Cataloging-in-Publication Data

Guardini, Romano, 1885-1968.
    And the Word dwelt among us : meeting the living God in
      scripture / Romano Guardini.
      p.   cm.
    Rev. ed. of: Word of God. 1963.
    ISBN 0-918477-75-1 (pbk. : alk. paper)
    1. Bible. N.T. John I, 1-18 — Meditations. 2. Bible. N.T. Romans
      VIII, 12-39 — Meditations. 3. Bible. N.T. Corinthians, 1st, XIII —
      Meditations. 4. Theological virtues — Biblical teaching — Meditations.
      I. Guardini, Romano, 1885-1968. Word of God. II. Title.
    BS2615.4.G8   1998
    225.6 — dc21   98-18698 CIP

98 99 00 01 02 03 10 9 8 7 6 5 4 3 2 1

Contents

Editor's Note: The biblical references in the following pages are based on the Douay-Rheims edition of the Old and New Testaments. Where applicable, quotations have been cross-referenced with the differing names and enumeration in the Revised Standard Version, using the following symbol: (RSV =).

∞

And the Word
Dwelt Among Us

∞

The Word of God

∞

In the beginning
was the Word,
and the Word was with God,
and the Word was God.

Through Him all things were made,
and without Him nothing was made
of all that was made.

In Him was life,
and the life was the light of men.
And the light shineth in darkness,
and the darkness did not comprehend it.

There was a man sent from God
whose name was John.
This man came for a witness
to give testimony to the light,
that all men might believe through him.

He was not the light,
but was to give testimony to the light.

And the Word was made flesh
and dwelt among us,
and we saw His glory, the glory as it were
of the only-begotten of the Father,
full of grace and truth.

John beareth witness to him and crieth out,
saying, "This is He of whom I spoke:
He who shall come after me
is preferred before me,
because He was before me."

And of His fullness we have all received,
and grace upon grace.
For the law was given by Moses;
grace and truth came by Jesus Christ.

No man hath seen God at any time:
the only-begotten Son,
who is in the bosom of the Father,
He hath declared Him.

John 1:1-18

◦∞◦

"In the beginning was the Word."

The beginning of St. John's Gospel, or, more exactly, the first
eighteen verses of his first chapter, the so-called Prologue, have
always made a particular impression upon the believer. Many
of its words touch the most hidden recesses of the spirit —
especially the very first: "In the beginning was . . ."

One of the eternal questions of mankind is indeed: "What
was in the beginning?" What was, in that beginning of time at
which we arrive — or believe that we can arrive — if we
retrace the hours and years and ages? What was, before anything had happened? What was the first thing that happened,
and how was it brought about? And what was the beginning
of being, the roots of things which we reach or believe that we
can reach when we grope through the structure of things, the
interaction of forces, the tissue of causes? What was, when
nothing as yet existed? What was the first thing from which
all else came, the essential, which gave its law to all the rest,
and from what power did it come?

Our consciousness seems to have two answers to these
questions. The first consists in explaining that there is no
answer, or, more exactly, that none is required, because the
question itself is false. There is no original cause and no first

or ultimate force, because beyond all that we fathom, a new riddle arises. Indeed, everything is in itself a closed cycle. The world is that which has no beginning or end, the whole and the all, the closed cycle, and no question can transcend it.

The other answer says: the movement of being is upward, from darkness and chaos into light and form. Hence in the beginning, there is voiceless being, blind necessity, unconscious urge, the primitive force.

Revelation replies: there is a beginning, and at the beginning stands the word and its creative act. We do not know as yet what this "word" means — for surely it means something special, and of that we shall have much more to say — but one thing is clear immediately: it is something bright, extended, free; a clearness of mind and a capacity for responsibility; not nature but spirit.

∞

In the beginning was the Word,
and the Word was with God,
and the Word was God.[1]

The beginning of which we have been speaking is that of the world, of which another passage of Scripture speaks, which also begins with this word — namely, the book of Genesis, whose first sentence reads, "In the beginning, God created the heavens and the earth."[2] But if we consider it carefully, the beginning of which the Prologue of St. John's Gospel speaks

[1] John 1:1.
[2] Gen. 1:1.

lies even beyond this. St. John does not mean the beginning of the world, but beginning itself. It is not so named because it is the origin of something that came later, but because it is before all that can ever be. It is analogous to the term *Lord* as applied by the Scripture to God. He is not Lord because there is something over which He rules, but He is Lord in Himself and of His very essence, the one absolutely free, powerful, self-possessed, and self-sufficient. So this beginning is prime reality and being; the eternal, fulfilled forever through itself and in itself.

We are told that an eternal speech goes on within this being. That which existed in itself in the beginning is not dumb but speaks — and this means also that it is spiritual, possessing the power of reason, and free.

The word is the fruit of speech. In the word, the hidden inner meaning is revealed. The truth appears and becomes a possibility and power in the structure of the situation. With man this word is a fleeting thing: scarcely has it been spoken when it dies away and remains only in the memory. The Word of which St. John speaks does not fade away, but is essential and real like God Himself. So it is said of this Word that it "was" in the beginning, was and is forever, and itself (of its essence) was God.

The history of the Word is recounted later, its creating and acting, its coming and dwelling in the world, its dealings, and its destiny. Hence it is a being. In the beginning, in the original existence, there is God and His Word, the one speaking and that which is spoken.

But what does God speak? That which is alone sufficient for Him to speak: Himself. He puts Himself, the all-inclusive abyss of meaning, the infinite power of being, into the expression of the Word.

And to whom does He speak this Word? Our word goes to another person, and, when it is perfect, to the one who belongs to us in love, the living "thou" of our "I." But to whom does the eternal Word of God go? There is no one who would be capable of receiving it — only He Himself. But how can He be His own hearer, His own "Thou"? If we correctly understand the Scripture, it tells us: God's Word, on its way to Him who would receive it, takes up a position in itself and becomes an ear that perceives. It is not the Word that goes to another, but that which has arrived in itself. Forming itself from the fullness of what is spoken, it becomes itself a "Thou."

So at the end of the Prologue, in the eighteenth verse, the Word is called by another name. There it is called "the Son," and He who speaks it, "the Father." "No one has seen God [in Himself] at any time. The only-begotten, God, who is resting in the bosom of the Father, He has brought us knowledge [of Him]."[3]

But even now we wish to emphasize what should be said after every sentence of what follows — namely, that nothing is explained by what we are saying here, not a fiber, not a nook of the mystery of which Revelation speaks. We can only trace its sentences, call attention to details, and draw connecting lines to that which is familiar to us, in order to come closer to its message.

Of this Word — let us use the more familiar Greek term — of this *Logos*, it is said that it was "with God" (*pros Theon*), that

---

[3] Cf. John 1:18.

is, "turned toward God." The next sentence repeats the statement;[4] hence it must be important.

It means that the *Logos* does not depart, as our human word does when it seeks the one who shall receive it and, if it does not find him, vanishes in space. The *Logos* does not depart; it remains. The word *remain* is dear to St. John. It means the opposite of parting, of leaving, of desertion and faithlessness; it means union and abiding, intimacy and faithfulness, fulfillment and eternity. Compare sentences such as this: "Let that remain in you which you have heard from the beginning. If that remains in you which you have heard from the beginning, then you will remain in the Son and in the Father. And this is the promise that He has promised us: eternal life."[5] In this way, the *Logos* remains in God.

Even more: He is "turned toward God" — a sacred expression. The Word, spoken and sent on its way, as is the nature of all speech, takes up a position, as it were, in itself. It becomes its own ear, is perceived and understood of itself, and turns back to Him who has spoken it. It becomes an "answer" (return word), an assurance of agreement in the common possession of truth. We must again refer to the last verse of the Prologue. There this remaining and returning is expressed by the phrase that the "only-begotten Son is resting in the bosom of the Father." Now the whole intimacy of the relation is revealed: the "answer" is faithfulness, closeness, love. And when we know St. John a little better, we feel a breath of his own experience passing through the words, for he was "the

---

4   "The same was in the beginning with God" (John 1:2).

5   1 John 2:24-25; similarly, 1 John 3:14, 17, 24; 4:13, 15-16.

disciple whom Jesus loved."[6] At the Last Supper, he rested on the bosom of the Master,[7] and that was probably not the only time. He knew something of the heart of God.

It is the triune life of God that is spoken of here; the manner in which there is "I" and "Thou" in God; the way in which He is person and yet has community.

Two faces appear, arising together and turned toward each other, the Father's and the Son's. The third, that of the Spirit, is not mentioned here. St. John speaks of Him in another connection, just as solemn as this one, namely, in the discourse of our Lord at the Last Supper. There the Lord says, "These things have I spoken to you, abiding with you, but the Paraclete, the Holy Spirit, whom the Father will send in my name, will teach you all things, and bring all things to your mind, whatsoever I shall have said to you." And again, "But I tell you the truth: it is expedient for you that I go; for if I go not, the Paraclete will not come to you; but if I go, I will send Him to you. But when He, the Spirit of truth, is come, He will teach you all truth. For He shall not speak of Himself, but . . . He shall receive of mine and shall show it to you."[8]

We cannot here attempt to penetrate these sentences. They would tell us that the mystery of God's speaking is accomplished in the Holy Spirit. That God speaks, and speaks in this way; that His Word has this reality, but does not become a second God; that it proceeds living and rational from the Father, but does not depart, turning about, as it were,

---

[6] John 19:26.

[7] John 13:23.

[8] John 14:25-26; 16:7, 13-14.

and turning to Him; that in God there is a true "I" and "Thou," and yet unity and oneness and complete intimacy — all this is possible only in the Spirit. But if we wish to perceive this mystery of the divine intimacy as a living impulse, we must read the close of the last discourse, the seventeenth chapter of St. John's Gospel. It is completely pervaded by the Holy Spirit.

∞

Through Him all things were made,
and without Him nothing was made
of all that was made.[9]

That of which we have been speaking took place in the primeval sphere of the Divinity. Now comes the account of the deeds and adventures of the *Logos*.

His first deed was the creation. In Genesis we read, "In the beginning, God created the heavens and the earth," and then the interior progress of this creation is recounted. But how does God create? By speaking. It is not by letting the world spring forth from Himself, or by externalizing Himself in it, or by imagining it; but by His word, His command. "God said, 'Let there be . . .' "[10] St. John tells us the deeper secret of that which Genesis shows us at work, for behind the word that turns outward in divine creation, there is the interior word of the divine life. The former is a free radiation of the latter, free because creation is not of necessity, but comes from God as deliberately willed action; because in the *Logos*, the eternal

[9] Cf. John 1:3.
[10] Gen. 1:3, 6, 14.

expression of the divine mind, all possibilities of divine crea-tion are likewise expressed. God creates through His eternal Word, the Father through the Son — and let us add — in the power of the Holy Spirit.

There is a clear and definite distinction between the world-concept of Revelation and all others. In the beginning, we find not that to which the present age reduces everything — mere nature with all the reserve, determinism, stuffiness, and even stupidity, which is implied in this concept — but the bright, free, responsive Word of the living God. From this everything proceeds. St. John emphasizes this — absolutely everything. Nothing that was made was made without it. There are no lateral channels of becoming, no other sources of being — nothing that is independent of God. In no sense is there an autonomous world, which by that very fact would necessarily be an evil one. Everything comes from God; every-thing comes from His Word. Whenever we meet something in the world which is estranged from God, denies Him, or op-poses Him, we are meeting something which, as a being, also originates from His word and has received from Him the very power by which it rebels against Him. Of itself it has only the evil will, the rebellious disposition. Nor is there a principle of evil, a force which of its nature always wills what is evil, but only the will which was created good and became unfaithful, the power that is capable of good but fell away from God.

Wherever man goes, he meets God's property. Nowhere is there a realm which essentially and rightfully belongs to an-other; nowhere are there enclaves of reality where man could confront what is really foreign. All is the property of God. Perhaps we must undergo certain periods of desolation, certain experiences of merciless wickedness in order to understand what that means. There are moments in which the words "Everything belongs to God, and what appears otherwise is only rebellion against Him" become the only support of our hope.

∞

In Him was life, and the life was the light of men.
And the light shineth in darkness,
and the darkness did not comprehend it.[11]

So the world was made, God's work through the *Logos*. Of this *Logos* it is now said that He is life and light. The two words belong together; they explain, interpret, and fulfill each other. The God who creates the world and whose power everywhere pervades the world is life. He abides in Himself, breathes and blooms from Himself, works from His own beginning, and, in working, belongs to Himself. This life is not dull, not a mere fermentation, urge, stream, or whatever the present day means by that word, but such that His nature can be expressed by the words "He is light."

The first letter of St. John, the echo of his Gospel, tells us, "And this is the message that we have received from Him and proclaim to you: that God is light, and there is no darkness in Him."[12] *Light* means clearness of mind, breadth of consciousness, freedom and responsibility, brightness and sublimity, grandeur and glory — in a word, "spirit"; spirit, not as our age

[11] 1 John 1:4-5.
[12] 1 John 1:5.

understands it, but "life." The light here spoken of is not merely consciousness, hard validity, dry concept, cold order, or overpowering law, but warmth, fruitfulness, a streaming and self-giving fullness, intimacy, closeness, and love. Out of this, the world was created, and where it seems contradictory, the will of man, into whose hand it was delivered, has spoiled it. So it is, and is it not a joy to be permitted to think this?

This life of the *Logos* "was the light of men." This does not mean merely the sun, which strikes the eyes of man and causes him to be able to perceive objects and go upon his way — yet it is this also. For the sight of our eyes is much more inclusive than the sense-perception of animals, because it reaches even into the spirit. The renewal of understanding, which is the task imposed upon us, the heirs of a dying age of reason, consists largely in rediscovering what the eye is: not merely the beginning but the half of all understanding; it consists in learning once again what true and complete seeing is — namely, the grasping of the original reality. Then we shall succeed also in the second half, the right comprehending and naming of the essence of things. When this seeing, which reaches from the surface of the body even into the spirit, is properly carried out, then things reveal themselves therein as truth — that is light. And now St. John says they cannot do this of themselves. Of their own nature, they would remain closed. They open to truth only in another which gives them the ability to do so, and this is the true light.

The Greeks had a presentiment of this when they spoke of the "idea." They said that the understanding of an object did not consist in our perceiving qualities and establishing proportions, but that it meant that what had previously been closed to us opened in the spirit as truth. But this it could do only in its eternal prototype, the idea. When the spirit had properly striven and the time was ripe, the idea would rise from the object, and in the idea, the object would be revealed; and this act of becoming light and transparent they said was the truth. In this way, they created a concept which later was ready at hand when St. John wished to explain the eternal nature of his Master, and which he used. The condition of all understanding, the light that reveals all things so that the spirit of man can behold, find direction, and satisfy itself with truth — that is the spiritual power of the eternal Word, the *Logos*.

It shines in the darkness. To begin with, all is darkness, voiceless being, locked in that which we call "earth" and "time," but everywhere the light of the *Logos* waits, ready to shine forth.

But then we read that the darkness did not comprehend the light. This darkness is evidently different from that of which we have just spoken. The former was the natural veiling of that which is not yet known, the darkness which bears the spark in itself; the latter has shut itself up within itself and refuses the light which comes from the *Logos*.

This refusal is sin. God created the world in such a way that the light of the *Logos* shall shine out for men from all that exists. Everything should be for them a living revelation and hence a way to God. Then each thing would be a call, an outstretched hand, a means of returning home, as we read in the letter to the Romans: "That which is known of God is manifest in them. For God hath manifested it unto them. For the invisible things of Him, from the creation of the world, are clearly seen, being understood by the things that are made;

[likewise] His eternal power also and His divinity."[13] Men were unwilling, and so a veil came over creation. Everything became rigid. Things shut themselves up, and directions were changed.

∞

There was a man sent from God
whose name was John.
This man came for a witness
to give testimony to the light,
that all men might believe through him.
He was not the light,
but was to give testimony to the light.[14]

The thought of the apostle began in the eternal existence of God, proceeded thence to the beginning of things and their creation, and then turned to the width of this world, the light that comes from the *Logos* and is everywhere. Now he enters upon the history of the explicit revelation in the moment before its final hour, when the precursor, John, appears and points to the Messiah.

The manner in which the apostle speaks of the Baptist has a particular character; we notice it again when the text later returns to him. John had come to point out the Messiah; that completed his task. At the moment when the Messiah appeared, John stepped back. His disciples, however, did not understand this self-effacement, but clung to him as their

---

[13] Rom. 1:19-20.
[14] John 1:6-8.

teacher and master. We perceive the possibility of such solidarity when the Gospels speak of the disciples of the Baptist. After the Baptist had been executed, the circle seems to have remained as a close community and to have set up the figure of their master in opposition to Jesus. The apostle attacks this attitude.[15] The movement must have been of considerable importance and long duration, for St. John's Gospel was written almost seventy years after the death of the Baptist.

In view of this, we can understand the peculiar emphasis of the sentences. John was indeed sent by God, a prophet who was to give testimony to the light and teach men to believe in it. But he was not himself the light, was not the essential revelation, as his disciples evidently maintained, but only the herald and precursor.

The following sentences of the text are closely connected with what precedes.

∞

"The true light that enlightens every man
was He who was to come into the world.
He was in the world,
and the world was made by Him,
and the world knew Him not.
He came unto His own,
and His own received Him not.
But as many as received Him,
He gave them power to be made the sons of God,
to them who believe in His name,

---

[15] Cf. John 3:26 ff.

> *who are born, not of blood,*
> *nor of the will of the flesh,*
> *nor of the will of man,*
> *but of God."*[16]

The light, whose rising signifies salvation, was not John, but He who was to come into the world. Usually the sentence is translated, "He was the true light that enlightens every man who comes into this world." But this changes the meaning. Actually the word *come* refers not to men but to the light, and so contrasts sharply with the claim of John's disciples.

At the same time, it expresses something tremendous, which we must take into the depths of our soul. The *Logos,* who is the eternal light, the expression of God Himself, whose fullness of wisdom and power has created and preserves all things, whose original idea stands behind all that is and makes it able to flame out in the spirit as truth — this *Logos* Himself appears as such in history.

This is something before which we must stand in amazement and whose enormity we must feel if we are to have a clear awareness of what Christianity means. That God's power of light lifts His own being eternally into knowledge is a truth that teaches us to adore; that everything in the world comes from it gives us holy confidence; that everywhere in things there waits the divine spark, ready to flame up as soon as a spirit of good will approaches it, fills us with gratitude and with remorse as well. All this is great, but our inner being responds to it with a certain readiness.

[16] John 1:9-13.

But now something quite different is stated: not only that this eternal power of light has created all things, pervades all things, and enlightens every willing spirit, but that it appeared in history as someone — at this definite time and no other; in that place, not elsewhere; with this particular nature and quality and not another. This is something of quite another order than that which has been previously recounted. And so the text leaves no doubt about it. The fact that the true light "is He who was to come into the world" is decisive for everything, faith and unfaith, salvation and perdition.

This choice is difficult, since the worse alternative seems more probable than the better one. When John was writing, he was an old man. Seventy years had passed since Christ had returned home to the Father — more than an average whole life-span. John had proclaimed the sacred truth and fought for it, had penetrated it by his thought, his prayer, and his life. But always there remained in him the overwhelming wonder about how that which *did* happen *could* happen: that the *Logos*, the light itself, the boundless fullness of wisdom and creative power, came into the world, that He stood in the world and shone, that He spoke, associated with men, acted, and yet was not received.

"The world was made through Him, and yet the world did not know Him." What the world was, it was through Him; it had received from Him the power to think, to will, to decide — and all this it used to resist Him. "He came to His own, and His own received Him not." He was the Lord. Things were His property; men, the members of His household. There was a close bond of relationship between Him and men, not only by right and authority, but interiorly, in that He had created them and loved them. The depths of their being should have yearned toward Him, as a moving object to its proper place, as kindred blood to its like — and yet when He came, they did not receive Him.

What happened is not only incomprehensible, but terrible; not only wrong, but, in a horrible way, contrary to nature. Something powerful and glorious — freedom — here became perverted. The final perfection of God's creation consists in the fact that He not only places His creature in true being, but sets it free to stand and move, to be the cause of its own activity, capable of decision and responsibility. This means the possibility of turning to God of its own accord, but also the possibility of not doing this. This should never have happened, but it did happen. How that could come to pass no one understands.

But if the *Logos* Himself stood in the world, if He had created the world and by His power kept it in existence, if He was the Lord and everything belonged to Him, then why did He permit that? Here again there is something mysterious, which, however, belongs to the inmost truth of Revelation: He had the power, but — dare we say it? — was not permitted to use it.

Whatever is of a low order forces its way immediately: bodily needs, movements of defense and protection, essential communications. The higher something rises, the more it loses the immediate force because it must pass through the spirit and the heart of man. The inmost being must open to it more and more purely. Very great and noble things have no immediate force at all, only their inner goodness and nobility. They appeal neither to natural urges nor to utility, neither to fear nor to ambition, or whatever the forces may be which arise spontaneously, but only to freedom, the depths of the heart, the heights of the spirit. Therefore they are wholly dependent on the responsibility of conscience and are defenseless in the world.

Nobility consists in perceiving the voice of that which is lofty and consequently powerless, and in defending it. This is true even in the world, and much more so in God. When the living light came into the world, it did not wish to blind and overthrow. It could have done so; that is shown by the mysterious events that punctuate the public ministry of Jesus: for instance, when He, at the moment when the raging mob at Nazareth was on the point of casting Him from the cliff, turned around and "passing through the midst of them, went His way";[17] when they wished to destroy Him, but did not dare to seize Him "because His hour had not yet come";[18] when, in the garden of Gethsemane, He asked the soldiers whom they were seeking and to their reply, "Jesus of Nazareth," answered, "I am he," and they fell to the ground.[19] We should recall, too, the incident of the fig tree, when He approached it in order to find fruit and, not finding any, cursed the tree, which promptly withered.[20] In Jesus we feel an incomprehensible power combined with perfect serenity. He releases this power when there is need of help or of a proof of goodness and truth, and then a miracle takes place. He never uses it to overawe or overthrow

[17] Luke 4:30.
[18] John 8:20.
[19] John 18:6.
[20] Matt. 21:19.

His opponents, to win over or stir up the people, or even to gain the assent of His audience more easily. It is a tremendous thing to see how He who possesses all power does not use it, so that the truth may appear only in the majesty of its meaning, and man may speak his "yes" to it quite freely, in no way compelled or even influenced.

The succeeding sentences of the Prologue can be understood only if we take them, not in isolation, but in their varied relations. They tell us what the *Logos* does for those who turn to Him readily. "He gives them power to become children of God." But the capacity to turn toward Him is given only to those who are "born not of blood, nor of the will of the flesh, nor of the will of man, but of God." Their readiness, their whole disposition comes not from nature or from the powers of the species or of their gender, but from above, from God. They have within them a new principle of existence, bestowed by God Himself. But if that is the case, they are already children of God.

Jesus Himself says that only the man who is already "of God" can perceive the sacred majesty of the Incarnate One, can hear His voice, understand His message, and receive Him as Savior. "You are from beneath; I am from above. You are of this world; I am not of this world. Why do you not understand my speech? Because you cannot hear my words. He who is of God hears the word of God. Therefore you do not hear it because you are not of God."[21] In this case, one thing is not earlier and the other later, but they are simultaneous, and the one through the other. He who receives the incarnate God is

[21] John 8:23, 43, 47.

given power to become the child of God; but no one can receive Him who is not already "born of God," that is, His child. In order to receive the *Logos*, a man must "hear His voice" and "understand His words"; but he can do that only if he has "the ear" for it, and that is equivalent to the new life itself. These sentences seem contradictory, but they are not. Neither are they the expression of inexact thinking or pious emphasis. Rather, they express something that cannot be said otherwise.

Let us recall the manner in which St. Augustine,[22] who is closely akin to the apostle John, speaks in the first chapters of his *Confessions*. There, too, one thing is not derived from another, but a whole appears, indeed the whole itself, the new life. Before the incarnate God, from Him and toward Him, this new life awakens when man wills, which he can do only when God grants that he will it. But He grants it to everyone who is ready, for all are to be saved. "Come to me, all," Jesus said.[23] The secret of free will and that of grace here flow inseparably into one.

∞

And the Word was made flesh
and dwelt among us,
and we saw His glory, the glory as it were
of the only-begotten of the Father,
full of grace and truth.

[22] St. Augustine (354-430), Bishop of Hippo and Doctor of the Church.
[23] Matt. 11:28.

And the Word Dwelt Among Us

John beareth witness to him and crieth out,
saying, "This is He of whom I spoke:
He who shall come after me
is preferred before me,
because He was before me."[24]

And now, prepared from the eternal beginning, from the origin of the world, from His operation in all of creation, and finally through the messenger who had been sent, the *Logos* steps into history.

The Word became flesh (became man) and dwelt among us — set up His tent among us, according to the expression of an ancient pastoral people. Again and again, we must tell ourselves that we are men of a later time; even worse, heirs of an age that has everywhere destroyed the meaning of the sacred words. So if we wish to understand the divine message correctly, we must first restore to its words that sacred newness which belongs to them by nature. Never, although men pondered it for thousands of years, could they comprehend and assimilate what God's words express. Always, no matter how often he may have heard or read them, they meet the hearer or reader as coming from God's holy hiddenness, at once judging and saving. They are "new" in their nature. This newness is never removed, but it can be covered by superficiality, neglect, and custom, and so receive a specious appearance of familiarity.

The sentence of which we are speaking we have heard very often, so perhaps we no longer perceive the immensity of its

[24] John 1:14-15.

message. It tells of the eternal Word, the *Logos*, the sum of all that we call "intelligence" and "being," first and originally the intelligence and being of God Himself, and also, in God, that of all that may exist or be created. This *Logos*, which is perfectly simple and yet immeasurably rich, is no order of forms and laws, no world of prototypes and arrangements, but *Someone*, He, the living Son of the eternal Father. We can stand before Him, face-to-face. We can speak to Him, and He answers; indeed, He Himself gives us the power to stand before Him, and He can grant our request. We can love Him, and He is able to give us a communion which reflects the intimacy in which He lies upon the bosom of the Father, and which St. John experienced when his Master permitted him to lay his head upon His heart. This fact established a contrast to everything which natural philosophy and piety can experience or invent. This *Logos*, this one and all, steps into history and becomes man. He does not merely touch a man, filling him with His life, lifting him in a vision beyond his own limits, creating a prophet who burns and shines for Him, but He Himself becomes man, so that we can say, "This is He!"

If St. John had been merely a prophet or a mystic, his spirit would have risen up in indignation against this thought. He would have sided with a non-incarnate *Logos* and so sided with his own mind, and would have said, "That cannot be. The eternal God, before whose power the world is as a breath, can never limit Himself in this way." At that time, there was a powerful intellectual movement which did maintain this — Gnosticism.

It is in opposition to this that St. John speaks: that the *Logos* did become man is the very essence of Christianity. If you remove this, then all depth of thought, all intellectual keenness, and all ecstasy that you may have is nothing. Even worse, it is false, corrupt, and destructive, for you have "dissolved Christ."

The eternal *Logos* steps into time and history, and He does this, if we may say so, for life and death, and remains irrevocably the one who came, who became man. He who shines in omnipotence takes up into the condition of His eternal divine life this particle of reality, the human nature united to Him. When you hear this, says St. John, when you feel what this means, when the danger of indignation rises in your mind, the danger of laughter in your feelings and senses, then you are standing before the decision whether you wish to be a Christian or not. If you wish it, if you overcome your resistance to "the scandal and the foolishness"[25] which threaten here, if you stand and confess your willingness, then you have truly "overcome the world,"[26] for you have broken the standards of the true and the good, the worthy and the right, which come from the world and have received new standards from God's Revelation.

The first letter of St. John, which is in many ways an echo of his Gospel, makes this decision very clear: "By this you know the spirit of God: every spirit that confesses Jesus Christ, who has come in the flesh, is of God; but every spirit that does not confess Jesus is not of God. And this is the nature of the anti-Christ, of whom you have heard that he is coming, and he is already in the world. You are of God, children, and have

[25] Cf. 1 Cor. 1:23.
[26] John 16:33.

overcome the world, for He who is in you is greater than he who is in the world. They are of the world; therefore they speak of the world, and the world hears them. We are of God. He who knows God hears us; he who is not of God does not hear us. By this we know the spirit of truth and the spirit of error."[27]

But because St. John is opposed to the Gnostics — who declared that matter, the body, and the senses were evil, doing exactly what the calumniators of Christianity accuse Christians of doing — and because he himself is a Christian and so does not despise the body, or the senses or matter, he raises a rampart against all such calumny by saying not merely, "The Word became man," but, "The Word became flesh."

And now his personal testimony comes forth: "We saw His glory, the glory as it were of the only-begotten of the Father, full of grace and truth."

Seventy years had passed since this happened, but it was as vivid as if it had been only the day before that He stood among them and they perceived His secret and beheld the revelation which He Himself was. At that time, they did not yet understand; they had not yet found their way to complete faith. That did not happen until the day of Pentecost. But what shone forth on that day through the power of the Spirit, they had received before.

The apostle speaks of the completion of what we call "Revelation": the epiphany of God in Christ. Christ not only spoke of God; He Himself was God. And the fact that He was God was clearly visible in Him. The spiritual soul in itself

[27] 1 John 4:2-6.

cannot be seen, but in a man's countenance, it becomes visible. The face is the spirit become visible. God in Himself cannot be seen — John will say this explicitly later on — but in the incarnate Christ, He became visible: Christ is the appearing, the manifest God. He had said so Himself, and John reports His word. When the disciple begged Him to show them the Father, of whom He had spoken so impressively, the Lord replied, "Have I been so long a time with you, and have you not known me, Philip? He who seeth me seeth the Father also."[28]

We must not soften these words. He does not mean merely that He proclaims the Father or by His disposition reminds us of Him, but that the Father, God, becomes visible in Him. This seeing is very important to the apostle; therefore He says, "We have seen His glory." And this is echoed by a passage at the opening of his first letter, which begins: "That which was from the beginning, which we have heard, which we have seen with our eyes, which we have looked upon, and our hands have handled, concerning the Word of life — the life was manifested; and we have seen and do bear witness, and declare unto you the life eternal, which was with the Father, and hath appeared to us. That which we have seen and have heard we declare unto you, that you also may have fellowship with us."[29]

We feel the insistence of the threefold repetition. It is not mere doctrine, but behind this seeing and hearing and handling, there lie the experiences of the life of the disciples, the

[28] John 14:9.
[29] 1 John 1:1-3.

countless impressions of daily association, the hours upon the Mount of the Transfiguration,[30] the risen Lord's standing in their midst, and the touching of His wounds.[31] The words express the solicitous striving to impress upon the hearer and unfold before him the reality of the statement: "He became flesh."

The glory of which John speaks does not mean just any glory, but that splendor of omnipotence which belongs to God alone, and which, in the course of sacred history, blazes up again and again: around the divine figure in the prophet's account,[32] or above the ark of the covenant,[33] or in the temple at the time of its dedication.[34] This glory, whose radiance the shepherds beheld in the field,[35] and which the Baptist saw gleaming from the opened heavens above Jesus as He emerged from the Jordan[36] — this was in Christ, and His disciples beheld it.

It was "full of grace and truth"; pure grace, sheer mercy and the opening of the heart of God; but also and always truth — both in one. When truth remains alone, it becomes hard. Here it is dissolved into mercy. When mercy remains alone, it becomes arbitrary. Here it is made firm in truth.

But nothing of this was in the Baptist. He only bore witness to it. He confessed that Jesus "overtook" him, although He

[30] Matt. 17:2; Mark 9:1; Luke 9:29.
[31] John 20:19, 27.
[32] Cf. Dan. 7:9.
[33] Exod. 40:36.
[34] 2 Paralip. 7:1 (RSV = 2 Chron. 7:1).
[35] Luke 2:8-9.
[36] Matt. 3:16; Mark 1:10.

"came after" him;[37] not because He was stronger or more efficient, but because He "was before" him, that is, from eternity. It is the same expression that we find Jesus using when He replies to the Pharisees who upbraid Him by telling Him that Abraham, to whom He refers, had lived before Him. His staggering statement is: "Before Abraham was, I am."[38]

∞

And of His fullness we have all received,
and grace upon grace.
For the law was given by Moses;
grace and truth came by Jesus Christ.[39]

Even earlier there was a hint of something which now comes out very strongly: the fullness in Christ. John had said that they had "seen His glory — full of grace and truth." This must have overwhelmed His disciples again and again: the fullness in Him, the profound depth of truth, the inexhaustible strength, the never-failing power of goodness, the divine creativity. What does it mean when He Himself says, "Come to me, all you who are weary and burdened, and I will refresh you"?[40] — He about whom the sick and crippled, the needy and abandoned were thronging. Before Him the disciples must have had the feeling: He can carry everything. From Him one

---

[37] Cf. John 1:15, 30.
[38] John 8:58.
[39] John 1:16.
[40] Matt. 11:28.

can obtain all things. He knows the truth that can solve every difficulty. His strength is equal to every need. One can trust Him for everything.

There is a beautiful expression of this experience, told also by St. John. After Christ's proclamation of the Eucharist in Capernaum, there came the great defection. As this affected even the inmost circle, Jesus asked the Apostles, "Will you also go away?" Peter, in his distress before the decision, was quite at a loss and cast himself upon the Lord: "Lord, to whom shall we go? Thou hast the words of eternal life."[41] "The words of eternal life" — that was the fullness that was in Him.

Of this fullness they "have all received" — constantly — "grace upon grace." The word is important. It expresses what they have received: not merely understanding, virtue, or righteousness, but grace; that which comes from the primary source of love, from the heart of God — warm, renewing, and creative; that which reaches beyond all distinction of merit and demerit, achievement and feebleness, the pure beginning.

This is emphasized once more. "For the law was given by Moses"; there was no need of a new law. "Grace and truth came by Jesus Christ." Again the sacred union of grace and truth, each in each. Grace comes from the intimacy of God, but this intimacy is that in which the *Logos* is the truth of the Father.

And at this point — a light seems to shine forth as we notice it — the Gospel for the first time uses the name Jesus Christ.

[41] John 6:68-69 (RSV = John 6:67-68).

∞

No man hath seen God at any time:
the only-begotten Son,
who is in the bosom of the Father,
He hath declared Him.[42]

And now the circle of this truly sacred text closes in a wondrous way. The thought returns to its starting point. God, in Himself, no man has ever seen. He is invisible. *Invisible* does not mean merely that He is a spirit — in this way, our soul, too, would be invisible — but that He is holy. This invisibility St. Paul expresses by saying that God "dwells in light unapproachable."[43] This light is His consuming holiness. No creature has ever come within its range. Only the Son knows of it. There the holy fullness of God's being becomes a revealed truth. When this occurs, God becomes Father and Son. And the Son, as the only one who knows the Father, turns lovingly toward Him. Jesus Himself speaks of this knowledge, saying in St. Matthew's Gospel, "No one knows the Father but the Son and he to whom it shall please the Son to reveal Him."[44]

Into the description of this knowledge flows the thought of what remained for the apostle the most precious thing in his life — the fact that his head had rested upon the bosom of his Master and that he felt the beating of His heart: "The only-begotten Son, God, who rests upon the bosom of the Father, has brought tidings of Him."

[42] John 1:18.
[43] 1 Tim. 6:16.
[44] Matt. 11:27.

It seems that nothing more remains to be said. This most sacred relation belongs to that sphere of which Cardinal Newman[45] speaks when he says, "God and my soul; nothing else in the world."

It is an immense picture that St. John paints in this brief text about Christ, stretching from eternity into time, spreading from the clearly defined actuality of the figure who walks along the streets of Palestine far out into the universe, living in the passing moment, yet cognizant of the beginning of all things, and even of the primeval beginning beyond time.

And it is no mere construction whose component parts are "the *Logos*" and "the flesh," but it is a living reality. No one has so plainly discerned the face of the Lord as St. John, who knew of the eternal fullness of wisdom of the *Logos*; no one has perceived so clearly the voice of the heart of Jesus as he who spoke of the eternal intimacy of Father and Son in God. He whom Christian symbolism portrays in the form of the eagle because he soared to the height of the eternal mysteries still remains "the disciple whom Jesus loved" and who lay upon the bosom of his Master. Men have charged John — and it is the most severe charge that could be brought against him — with being no true evangelist, no simple messenger of the reality of Jesus, but a "mystic" and a "thinker," one who buries himself in experiences and fabricates webs of thought. Some have even dared to say that he betrayed the plain truth of Jesus to the syncretistic learning and piety of the philosophers and the religious concepts of the time.

---

[45] John Henry Newman (1801-1890), English theologian and spiritual writer.

These statements are based upon a disbelief which does not wish to admit that Christ is the Son of God, and also upon a kind of sentimentality which considers pure Christianity something edifying, but childish and idyllic. Those who speak in this way have forgotten what *Revelation* means — the self-revelation of the living God at the moment of its ultimate manifestation — and they wish to prescribe for Him what He must be.

God is neither universal reason nor religious mystique. He is *He,* as He Himself said at the moment when He first mentioned His name: "And God said to Moses, 'I am who I am.' And He added, 'You shall say to the Israelites, the I-am has sent me to you.' "[46] Christ is neither the religious genius, nor the intimate friend of man, nor the founder of a religion, but the incarnate Son of this God. And to have faith means to receive from Him the measure of that which He is and to break one's own measure.

It is of this Christ that John speaks. So we must do what the Christian always has to do: change the order of things, give up the old starting point and seek a new one, put away our old measures and learn to use the new. It is not that John paints a picture of Christ which corresponds to his own nature as a theologian and mystic, and that scholars can now sit down and examine what the reality is, but John had met Christ. He had lived with Him. He was overpowered by that which Jesus was. He did not understand, and yet he remained with Him and stood beneath the Cross to the end. At the message of the women, he ran to the grave and became aware of the mystery

[46] Exod. 3:14.

of Easter. He experienced the descent of the Holy Spirit, and in that light, his eyes were opened. Until the end of his long life, he pondered about who this was whom he had encountered at that time, this man so simple and so immense, so close and yet always remote, who had gone in and out among them for a short time and yet was the Eternal One.[47]

John did not imagine this, but experienced it, and then he searched for ways of expressing it — just as the others tried to do, each in his own way, Mark, Matthew, Luke, and Paul. To do this, he employed not only the thoughts of the Old Testament about the creative word of God, but also those which the Greeks had prepared and expressed. What these had guessed, seeking and never reaching their goal as they spoke of the Logos, was now fulfilled in Him. As St. Paul had said on the Areopagus, "As I went about viewing your sanctuaries, I found an altar with the inscription: 'To an unknown God.' That which you worship without knowing, I proclaim to you."[48]

This is how it is, and all else is unbelief — unbelief and presumption. We cannot pass judgment upon Christ. We cannot say the apostle speaks the truth on this point, but on that point, he is under Hellenistic influence. If we do this, we take away Revelation and therewith the foundation of all that is called Christianity. We cannot by our own powers pass judgment upon Revelation, but can only receive from it what then becomes the content of our Christian thinking.

But we must let it be a real revelation, let it speak freely and receive all that it tells. The Christ of present-day scholarship

[47] Acts 1:21.
[48] Acts 17:23.

is empty and insignificant. We cannot believe in Him, and He does not bring salvation to anyone. Yet the Christ of faith has largely become atrophied, grown small and sentimental. But Christ is the figure in whom we shall "conquer the world";[49] hence He must be greater than the world, and that means greater than all. The Christ who lives in the customary thinking, speaking, and praying of our day is not so. In that Christ, there is not the fullness of Revelation, but only certain of its words and events, and, for the rest, the image of a custom.

If Christianity is to be renewed, this can be brought about only by a return to its root; that means to Revelation. We must place ourselves before this, must put aside all preconceived ideas, all portraits of art, all habitual attitudes, and must open our souls, perceive with our inner ear, behold with our inner eye what proceeds from there — trait by trait, event after event, word upon word, in Matthew and Mark and Luke, in Paul and John. Then a concept will grow up, of which we can perhaps not even say that it is an image — something immense that mocks our every measure; a Being who breaks apart all we are accustomed to and yet touches our innermost soul; He, Jesus Christ — the Lord — Lord by nature, who is who He is, Lord of His being, elevated above all judgment on our part, and by this very fact, our salvation. For what would be the good of a savior whom we had fathomed and stamped with our approval?

When this has taken place and all that is customary has been shattered, we may begin to consider how this and that may be, how the picture painted by Matthew is related to that

---

[49] Cf. John 16:33; 1 John 5:4.

of Paul. Then we shall once again perceive the depths of meaning in the traditional doctrines; the customary formulas will begin to glow, and everything that the Church says will become our own in an entirely new fashion.

Of course, something else is also necessary — prayer. The Christ of whom Revelation speaks "was yesterday, is today, and will be for all eternity."[50] The way to Him does not lead merely over books and reports, but immediately from us to Him — no, rather, originally and essentially from Him to us — passing through everything. So we must call upon Him so that He may reveal Himself to us. What He did to Paul on his way to Damascus[51] was, in prophetic greatness, something that He can do to each one of us according to the measure of our smallness and His grace.

---

[50] Cf. Heb. 13:8.

[51] Acts 9:2 ff.

∞

The Yearning of Creation

∞

Therefore, brethren,

*we are debtors, not to the flesh, to live according
to the flesh. If you live according to the flesh,
you shall die; but if, by the Spirit,
you mortify the deeds of the flesh, you shall live.*

*For whosoever are led by the Spirit of God,
they are the sons of God. You have not received the
spirit of bondage again in fear; but you have received the
spirit of adoption of sons, whereby we cry, "Abba (Father)."*

*For the Spirit Himself giveth testimony to our spirit,
that we are the sons of God, and if sons, heirs also;
heirs indeed of God, and joint-heirs with Christ, if we
suffer with Him, that we may be also glorified with Him.*

*For I reckon that the sufferings of this time are
not worthy to be compared with the glory to come,
that shall be revealed in us.*

*The expectation of the creature waiteth
for the revelation of the sons of God.*

For the creature was made subject to vanity,
not willingly, but by reason of Him who made it subject
in the hope that the creature also shall be delivered
from the servitude of corruption into the liberty
of the children of God. We know that every creature
groaneth and travaileth in pain, even till now.

And not only every creature, but we ourselves,
who have the firstfruits of the Spirit, groan within ourselves,
waiting for our adoption, the redemption of the body.

For in the meantime, we are saved only in hope.
But hope that can be seen is no hope, for if we see
something, how can we hope for it? But if we truly hope
for that which we see not, we shall wait in patience.

Likewise the Spirit also helpeth our infirmity.
For we know not what we should pray for as we ought;
but the Spirit Himself asketh for us with unspeakable
groanings. And He who searcheth the hearts knoweth
what the Spirit desireth, because He intercedeth
for the saints according to God.

And we know that to them who love God,
all things work together unto good, to such as,
according to His purpose, are called to be saints.
For those He foreknew, He also predestined
to be made conformable to the image of His Son,
that He might be the firstborn among many brethren.
And those He predestined, He also called.

And those He called, He also justified.
And those He justified, He also glorified.

What shall we then say to these things?
If God is for us, who is against us?
He who spared not even His own Son,
but delivered Him up for us all,
will He not also give us all things with Him?

Who shall accuse the elect of God? God who justifieth.
Who is he who shall condemn? Christ Jesus who died,
who is risen again, who is at the right hand of God,
who also maketh intercession for us.

Who, then, shall separate us from the love of Christ?
Shall tribulation, or distress, or famine, or nakedness,
or danger, or persecution, or the sword?

But in all these things, we overcome,
because of Him who hath loved us.

For I am sure that neither death, nor life,
nor angels, nor principalities, nor powers,
nor things present, nor things to come,
nor might, nor height, nor depth,
nor any other creature shall be able
to separate us from the love of God,
which is in Christ Jesus our Lord.

Romans 8:12-39

◇◇

Deep within each man, there lives
the consciousness that something must happen to him, that
this present existence is not the real and true one, that it must
become new and different and so attain to its proper reality.

If one should ask him, he would not be able to say how this
is to be, yet he waits for it with a hope that he perhaps does
not admit even to himself. This hope is often mistaken about
its own meaning. Then man thinks that what he is waiting for
is the coming day or the spring or some encounter or a change
in circumstances. But he is mistaken. The change for which
he is really waiting does not consist in this — that he will
learn tomorrow to control himself better than today, that his
next work will be more successful than the last, that he will
rise to success and power or will find the person whose love
can wholly rouse and fill him. These things are fundamentally
merely changes within a similar situation. What he desires is
the real transformation, the genesis of something entirely new,
from which man would at last receive his proper self.

But are these not fantasies — beautiful, profound, and ultimately vain imaginations of human longing?

No, to appeal to this desire, to interpret it, to promise that
it shall be fulfilled, indeed that the fulfillment has already

begun and is being consummated through the ages — this is the meaning of the "good news," the gospel. We shall learn this from one of the deepest and richest texts of Scripture, the eighth chapter of the letter that St. Paul wrote to the congregation at Rome.

∞

In the preceding chapter of his letter, the apostle Paul had spoken of the lost state of man, of sin and remoteness from God. Through his own vivid experience, he had shown that man cannot overcome these things either through the law of the Old Testament or through any efforts of his own strength, but that only grace in Christ could bring salvation.

Then he continues: "Therefore, brethren, we are debtors, not to the flesh, to live according to the flesh. If you live according to the flesh, you shall die; but if, by the Spirit, you mortify the deeds of the flesh, you shall live. For whosoever are led by the Spirit of God, they are the sons of God. You have not received the spirit of bondage again in fear; but you have received the spirit of adoption of sons, whereby we cry, 'Abba (Father).' For the Spirit Himself giveth testimony to our spirit, that we are the sons of God, and if sons, heirs also; heirs indeed of God, and joint-heirs with Christ, if we suffer with Him, that we may be also glorified with Him."[52]

St. Paul speaks of the flesh and of the spirit, and it is important that these words be given their true meaning. By *the flesh* he does not mean the body in contrast to the spiritual

[52] Rom. 8:12-17.

soul. This has been imputed to him, and so he has been accused of being a despiser of the body, whereas he is the very one who has proclaimed the message of the Christian body, of man in his entirety. *Flesh* means body and soul together; impulse, reason, will, and energy; the whole man and all his works; knowledge, art, and culture — in a word, earthly existence as it is of itself.

By *spirit* he does not mean the disembodied soul or mere reason, but that which had come to men in such a tremendous manner on the first Pentecost, the Holy Spirit with His creative power, and all that which this power brings forth and penetrates. And the either-or of which he speaks does not demand that man shall destroy the body for the sake of the spirit. There was even then a heresy which held this opinion and which St. Paul himself, and especially St. John, combated, namely, Gnosticism. But St. Paul's alternative proclaims the struggle between the life which the Holy Spirit produces in man and that which comes from the world and is circumscribed by it.

St. Paul says that through faith in the gospel, we are committed to a new way of life. Herein we shall not serve what is earthly, for in that way, we shall die. Here speaks the deep experience of the ancients — that everything passes away, even what is greatest and most beautiful. No one becomes completely human who does not in some way reach this experience: that everything passes away and that nothing which is itself perishable can save us from this transitoriness. Man is not saved from death when a child is born to him, for this child in turn must die. He is not saved from perishing if he leaves a great work, for, in its time, this also shall perish. He does not overcome the powers of annihilation if he is remembered by men for his noble deeds, for, in time, these men will also forget.

We must be honest and not take away the meaning of the words. If transitoriness is to be overcome, this can be done only by means of something which does not pass away — and not merely in the sense in which poets use the words, but in actual truth. St. Paul says that this something exists: it is Christ. When you turn to Him and unite yourselves to Him, a new life awakens in you through the Holy Spirit, a life over which death has no power.

In this life, you have a new relation to God, a new rank and a new right. You are His sons. No longer merely sons of men, of your parents, your clan, and your people, but of God. And the Spirit is the sacred breath which blows from Him through you, and the will that comes from the Father and guides you.

In this way, you are raised above the natural order by which everyone is bound. Of course, there is the distinction between those who rule and those who serve, the independent and the dependent, and the greater distinction between the liberal and the servile-minded man. Paul, with his strong individualism, would be the last to deny this. But he would add that these differences lie within a great universal limitation, that of earthly existence as such. Every man is bound by this: his body through the laws of nature, his emotions through the impulses, his reason through uncertainty and error, his will through the power of evil, and his whole life through death. This subservience also includes fear. Everyone, even the bravest, feels this — the fear of the creature in an existence with which it is fundamentally in disharmony.

But the Spirit has raised us to a new status in making us brethren of Christ. As a result of this, we have a new disposition, that of children. The new spirit within us speaks directly to the holy, eternal God, and in this face-to-face, there is no longer fear, but freedom and confidence. The word we speak in the Lord's Prayer, "Abba (Father)," is the expression of the redeemed existence. How do we know that? First of all, from the word of God, which we receive in the obedience and confidence of faith. But we could not receive and retain it, it would be a "folly and a scandal"[53] for us, if there were not something in the depths of our hearts that assured us of its truth. This results from the witness in which the voice of the Holy Spirit joins our redeemed spirit.

The Holy Spirit is a great mystery. He is the intimacy and freedom of God. He is His holy animation. We are told that God, knowing and expressing Himself, generates an eternal "Thou," the Son, and thereby becomes the Father. But this Son does not separate from the Father, depart, and become an independent God (which would cause everything to fall into falsity and destruction); He "remains" with the Father, "turns toward Him," "lies upon His bosom," as St. John says, and the unity of God is preserved — indeed, receives in this holy plenitude its peculiar force. This is the work of the Holy Spirit.

Again it is He who brings it about that the Father, in keeping the Son with Him, does not suppress Him; that the Son is not immature, unreal, the mere shadow of a greater one, but lives in the clarity and power of a free self, the equal and

[53] Cf. 1 Cor. 1:23.

responding "Thou" of the speaking "I." So the Spirit is the intimacy of God.

And He is divine humility. He does not seek Himself. He seems to have no content of His own, to desire nothing but that the eternal God may possess the dignity of fatherhood and the beauty of sonship, and that both, Father and Son, may be in possession of each other and be one. He is the selfless one, the lover truly so called, and therefore He is absolute power.

This Spirit also effects the intimacy of the redeemed life. He makes man to be truly the child of God, without blurring the clear distinction between creator and creature. He gives him the true life that comes only from God, pure grace, but, by that very fact, so much man's own that only now does he become wholly himself. He reassures man of this in the inmost depths of his soul, so that it becomes a powerful certainty in him and no shadow of doubt remains. Man's own spirit, that which is new in him, comes to a joyous self-realization and says, "So it is."

What is described in this way is the particular experience of the apostle Paul and is not granted to many. But everyone who believes bears within himself the reality of which that experience speaks. Everyone who believes is assured by the Spirit in the depths of his being that he is a child of God. Every believer's "own spirit" perceives this assurance and agrees with it, even though the witness and the answer do not become an open experience, but remain hidden in the depths. If this were not the case, he could not believe the message; the objection of his earthly reality would be too strong. Without knowing it, he believes from the inner witness of the Spirit.

This being a child of God is a serious thing. It gives us rights. It makes us heirs of God. His property belongs to us — His holiness, His life, His kingdom — and since He is one and completely simple, that means He Himself belongs to us. The true heir is Christ. He will be the Lord of the new creation, and we shall be co-heirs with Him, so that He will be "the firstborn among many brethren."[54]

Of course, we must also be ready to share His destiny, to experience what He experienced when He, who had come from Heaven, lived on earth. If we are willing to endure the contradiction of "the flesh" against the Lord of the spirit, we shall also receive a share of His glory.

∞

For I reckon that the sufferings of this time
are not worthy to be compared with
the glory to come, that shall be revealed in us.
For the expectation of the creature
waiteth for the revelation of the sons of God.
For the creature was made subject to vanity,
not willingly, but by reason of Him who made it subject
in the hope that the creature also shall be delivered
from the servitude of corruption
into the liberty of the children of God.
For we know that every creature
groaneth and travaileth in pain, even till now.[55]

[54] Rom. 8:17, 29.
[55] Rom. 8:18-22.

These sufferings are real, and they are bitter, but they lose their weight when the Spirit assures us of the glory which is ripening in us and shall one day be revealed. In these sentences and those that follow them, there speaks the triumphant greatness of the Christian message about man. It says that man is a mystery. The part of him that we see and hear is a transitory earthly being, but within him lives something that comes from the Spirit. In all his existing, acting, and experiencing, in all feeling, possessing, and privation, something else lies veiled, oppressed, contradicted, and yet always there. This shall one day be revealed. It is God who actually reveals Himself, He whose Revelation is truth. But He wills to make man so that the concept of Revelation applies to him also. He, too, is a veiled meaning, a fullness of actuality ripening in secret, someday to come forth into life.

That a person can be Christian is something that also must be believed. I must believe in my own Christianity, and that is often difficult, for everything contradicts it. But one day it shall appear, and then faith shall pass away. Everything shall be present and open to our sight.

Now comes the tremendous thought: the whole of creation is turned toward this mystery in man, this interior becoming, struggling, and unfolding. It is a waiting, and the attention of this waiting is not directed immediately toward God, but toward man, for the way of creatures to God goes through man. Their hearts and heads should be in him; he should lead them to God, and, in him, all creation should be blessed. But he turned away from God and dragged creatures with him. So the curse struck them also, together with him, kept them at a distance from God, subjected them to transitoriness and vanity, and brought it about that there was no longer an answer to the questions *whence, whither, why,* and *for what purpose*.

Nature itself was not guilty, for it cannot have guilt of its own. It exists for the sake of man and receives its meaning from him; hence it was from him that the disaster came upon it. And now it waits for the blessing of salvation to come about in him, so that it may share therein through him. From all sides, a silent, anxious expectation is directed toward man.

It reminds us of some old pictures of the nativity: the Child lies shining in the manger, and all about Him, eyes are gazing upon the radiance — the eyes of the Blessed Mother and the faithful protector, of the shepherds and the beasts — and it seems as if the darkness were full of life and were pressing in from all sides. It is almost like that in the present case. In man who believes, there is an opening, a beginning; a fire is burning, a light is shining, and the whole wide world presses toward this blessed beginning, hoping that it may also be caught up in it. If the new life triumphs in man, it shall also triumph in nature. Then the "service of corruption," the law of dissolution and hopeless death shall fall away from the world, and it shall attain freedom.

This freedom means more than the possibility of doing one thing or another; indeed, it is not a freedom of action, but of being — that freedom which is truth. It becomes actual when that which is hidden comes to light, when the insignificant captive of natural laws, the child of man, becomes the child of God and participates in the glory of his Father. And let us take the word *glory* in its full significance. It does not mean just any beauty or radiance, but something very definite, the light of the apparition of God upon Mount Sinai, over the ark of the covenant, in the faces of the prophets, and, finally, the fullness of light and majesty of the risen Christ.

In this we shall share, as heirs of that which belongs to God. It is for this that creation waits. The condition of man in time is that of a blessed life which waits until it can bring to light that new life which is developing within. This is also the condition of creation. So St. Paul says that we groan and are in travail, and the whole of creation with us. Earthly existence, existence in time, is pain and travail, an urge toward the birth of a life that shall transcend all that belongs to earth and time, because the sacred seed has come from beyond all this.

∞

And not only every creature, but we ourselves
who have the firstfruits of the Spirit,
groan within ourselves, waiting for our adoption,
the redemption of the body.
For in the meantime, we are saved only in hope.
But hope that can be seen is no hope,
for if we see something, how can we hope for it?
But if we truly hope for that which we see not,
we shall wait in patience.[56]

The thought returns to man. Everything human shall also become the starting point of a new birth. But while creation is without knowledge or voice, we have become knowing through the Spirit, the inner light, the inner breath. So "we

[56] Cf. Rom. 8:23-25.

groan within ourselves," that what is in process of becoming, our adoption as sons of God, may be accomplished. Through faith and Baptism, it has begun. We are really children of God, but only children, immature. We have neither attained our freedom nor received our inheritance. That will take place only when we come of age, one day, in the "revelation of the sons of God."

And now another bold step: this revelation will be the redemption of our body. No other New Testament writer has ever dared to say anything like that, to define Christian maturity, the completion of our existence and that of the world, hence the end of all things, as the redemption of our body. It must be an evil desire to distort things that is responsible for regarding St. Paul as the enemy of the body and of human life, whereas he is the very one who has carried the body into eternity. Not only the spiritual soul shall enter into eternal life — one could almost say that the Christian message was not necessary for that, because that idea can be found in Plato[57] — but the whole man. The fact that man shall become eternal, that his body also shall attain to fellowship with God and shine in holy life: this has been revealed to us by Christ. But that is not all: Christ accomplished it by His Incarnation and Resurrection and made it possible for us all.

This is the Christian teaching about man, and St. Paul is the one who really proclaimed it. He is the prophet of the resurrection of the body, of the eternalized man, just as he, more than anyone who speaks in the New Testament, is the prophet of the risen Christ, who appeared to him on his way

[57] Plato (427-347 B.C.), Greek philosopher.

to Damascus and revealed to him the divine glory of His body. It is this glory which, by a creative sharing, continues its operation in the body of redeemed man.

But all this is still veiled, waiting, and in the process of becoming. Of a woman who has conceived and who awaits the time when the life growing within her shall come into the light, we sometimes use the phrase "she is expecting." This is the meaning that is suggested by the way in which St. Paul speaks of the expectation of man and of creation. It implies confidence in the promise that has been given and also a silent knowledge of that which is growing in secret. This expectation lives by the word of God and also from its own deepest inner being, assured by the Holy Spirit.

Christian hope is the confidence of man that he shall attain this new life, shall become a partaker of the maturity and dominion of the sons of God. At present it is contradicted by everything: the ugliness and evil within us, the constant failure, the meanness and misery and hopelessness of existence. In view of all this, confidence seems folly, and for that very reason, it must be *hope*, trust in that which is not seen, and of which we are certain beyond all uncertainty; "hope," as St. Paul says in the same letter, "against all hope."[58]

And it is patience. Thereby genuine hope differs from the fanciful. The latter flares up and collapses, since it comes from the surge of emotion and the fleeting images of fantasy. But genuine hope grows from reality, the interior, new reality based upon the Spirit. Therefore it is strong enough to resist the contradiction of the old reality and to overcome its resistance.

[58] Cf. Rom. 4:18.

For reality has one special quality: it is tough. It allows growth only in those things which sustain themselves within it. This persevering, this overcoming of reality by the power of endurance, is patience. How strong and full of conquering power is the blessing with which the explanations of the letter conclude: "May the God of hope fill you with all joy and peace in believing, that you may abound in hope and in the power of the Holy Spirit."[59]

∽

Likewise the Spirit also helpeth
our infirmity. For we know not
what we should pray for as we ought;
but the Spirit Himself asketh for us
with unspeakable groanings.
And He who searcheth the hearts
knoweth what the Spirit desireth, because
He intercedeth for the saints according to God.[60]

It is the Spirit who has placed the seed of the new life in us, and it is He who helps it to hope — to hope and even to live. What came into being through Him can live only through Him. The life, at once human and divine, was awakened in Mary through the descent of the Holy Spirit and the overshadowing power of the Most High,[61] and in the power of this same Spirit, Christ lived and completed His work. The Christian

[59] Rom. 15:13.
[60] Rom. 8:26-27.
[61] Luke 1:35.

life is patterned after the life of Christ. It begins through the Holy Spirit; in Him it lives and grows, struggles and hopes.

The first movement of this life, its breath, so to speak, is prayer. Of ourselves we do not know how we should pray. The Spirit teaches us. The meanings of these terms blend very beautifully. The Spirit is the "breath." The Holy Spirit is the breath of God. So it is He who teaches the new life in us to breathe, that is, to pray. Indeed, it is He Himself who breathes in us, and since it is the breath of an imprisoned life, oppressed by darkness and closeness and contradiction, this breath becomes a sighing for deliverance and consummation.

What was said before about the groaning of creation and our own, in the developing of the new life, here continues in a divine way. It is the Spirit Himself who longs within us for the consummation. The eternal care of His love, of His whole being which is love, is set upon this — that the sacred birth in God, the Father's self-expression in the Son and the turning of the Son to the Father, shall be carried out in the truth of a free personality and the union of an eternal abiding. The Spirit's work in time is, through the mystery of grace, to bring about the birth of the new life in the brethren of Christ.

How good is the message that the Spirit Himself breathes and prays and sighs in us! It would be a grievous thing if this growing and becoming were to lie in our ignorant, careless hands. How eternally good that He, our advocate, our comforter, has made it His own work.

Constantly, deep within us, in the growing-center of our being, the prayer of the Spirit goes on. Constantly the breath of His prayer ascends to the Father. And when we ourselves pray, whatever has value in this poor, inadequate prayer, comes from Him. His prayer reaches God. The meaning of His sighs is understood by God even if we ourselves do not yet understand it. We should include it in the conscious practice of our prayer, but it will always be deeper than this. It will always be true that God, the Father, understands it better than we do. He can do that, for He is the one who "searcheth the hearts." Another passage tells us that "the Spirit searcheth all things, even the depths of divinity."[62]

We see how wonderfully close to God the gospel brings man. It speaks of the inner depth of man — the new and holy depth, not the natural — in almost the same way as of the inner depth of God. He who lives in the mystery of the redeemed soul and in the abyss of God's holiness is — with the inviolable distinction that exists between God and His creature — the same Holy Spirit. What He desires is known to the Father. For the Spirit is the intimacy in which God lives within Himself. He also becomes the intimacy of man, for Jesus said that He would send Him as our comforter, our advocate, the one who brings it about that we are not left orphans.[63]

For us also He is closeness — the language of the Church calls Him "the bond," "the kiss." And it is not accidental that the word *saints* appears in this connection. We use this word of those great and extraordinary ones to whom the Church awards the glory of being invoked and venerated, but the Scripture uses it to denote all those who believe and are baptized — those in whom the Holy Spirit breathes.

---

[62] Cf. 1 Cor. 2:10.

[63] John 14:18; 16:7.

∞

And we know that to them who love God,
all things work together unto good,
to such as, according to His purpose,
are called to be saints.
For those He foreknew, He also predestined
to be made conformable to the image of His Son,
that He might be the firstborn among many brethren.
And those He predestined, He also called.
And those He called, He also justified.
And those He justified, He also glorified.[64]

In this passage is a single confirmation penetrating ever more deeply, growing ever more powerful and more joyful. The text begins, "And we know": not by our reason, not through some intellectual insight or practical wisdom, not through a mystical sense of security, which can always arise from religious absorption, but through that inner voice of the Holy Spirit of which we have spoken. To know that God makes "all things work together unto good" to those who love Him is a certainty that endures through all experiences and considerations.

The good which is spoken of here is the development of the new man. This is aided not only by fortunate dispensations, but by "all things." Even earthly ideas of the development and perfection of the personality can be far-reaching, and can include sorrow as well as happiness, but if they go too far, they become unreal. If they stay with reality, they soon reach the boundary where the purely destructive begins. But

---

[64] Rom. 8:28-30.

the certainty of which St. Paul speaks excludes nothing. It knows that absolutely everything that happens serves the inner development.

But again, and the reader must not be annoyed if we distinguish again and again — for it is a question of the very heart of the Christian message, and all depends on our making the meaning of the much misused words very clear — all things must serve the inner development, not because it comes irresistibly from the seed nurtured by powerful men, but because God's Providence never fails.

But the mystery has two sides. The persons spoken of are those "who love God" and at the same time those whom He has "called" according to His will. The first statement alone could mean that it is a question of the human heart's capacity of loving, and this would again reduce everything to an earthly level. The second could give us the impression that it is a question of an arbitrary choice, and would make man the plaything of a divine whim. In fact, it is both a call of pure grace, and, at the same time, the interior readiness of the heart, just as we can translate the Christmas message of the angels,[65] "Peace to men who are pleasing to God because His grace has chosen them," and also, "Peace to men who are pleasing to God because they are of good will." From this mystery results the Providence which brings it about that whatever may happen, even what is most incomprehensible and destructive, blends with the inner development.

And now this idea of pure grace, which has no conditions but itself, unfolds to its full power. The mystery is so great that

[65] Luke 2:14.

it can become dark and oppressive. We cannot penetrate it, but must take care that it is placed in its proper order.

In the letter to the Romans, we find a demonstration which most completely demolishes every claim that the law of the Old Testament might put forward to retain its validity, but also every claim which man's own will and accomplishments might make to work out his own salvation. It is true that the Old Testament also rested upon grace and demanded of man cooperation with the living God; but in other respects, it consisted largely of regulations about what should and should not be done — namely, the law — and the promises were bound up with its fulfillment. Repeatedly these words occur: "If you do this, you shall live."[66] Much that was found in this law was a matter of morality and piety, which always retain their significance, but essentially it was directed to the realization of sacred history and prepared for the coming of the Messiah, either by opening the hearts of men for Him, or, as the letter to the Romans says, by their inability to fulfill it, revealing to them their own helplessness.

But living by the law had brought about such a consciousness of righteousness and security that the Christians were in danger of adopting this consciousness together with the obligations of the law. In opposition to this, St. Paul says, "All this is past and gone. What matters now is not the law and its fulfillment, but the grace of God in Christ and faith in Him, life under the guidance of the Holy Spirit and in communion with the Savior." This renunciation of the law includes another. In itself the law was bound up with sacred history, as

[66] Cf. Deut. 30:16.

brought about by God; but it appealed so strongly to the will
and the accomplishment of man that it constantly threatened
to slip into natural morality and propriety. This, too, St. Paul
attacks. It is not that he places little value upon natural virtue;
rather he affirms that the essential thing with which the
gospel is concerned cannot arise from that. It comes from God,
grows through the operation of His Spirit, and is appropriated
by man in faith, love, and obedience. But herein lives all that
is magnanimous and strong in him. "I live, now not I, but
Christ liveth in me."[67]

Here all that has previously been said about the new life
becomes a living disposition. We can sum up its nature in two
statements. He who operates is God, not man; everything is a
gift; pride and also the fear of being obliged to bring about the
effect oneself no longer have any place. Everything is open
and selfless. But, at the same time, man must cast into this
freedom all that he possesses of readiness, of nobility, of power
to act and boldness to accomplish; nothing is too good or too
much. He who has received all must also give all.

From this point of view, we understand Paul's following
sentences.[68] What we are concerned with does not come from
the inner source of human life, nor from the depths of the
world, but from the mystery of the free divine decree, which is
impenetrable, because freedom is God's self — God, who depends upon the world for nothing, but is its creator and Lord.
That is the source of the hope of which we have spoken — for
those whom God has foreknown before all time, before all

[67] Gal. 2:20.

[68] See next page: "What shall we then say to these things? . . ."

earthly conditions, before all willing and ability and action of their own. These He has "predestined" to that holy becoming whose nature consists in being "conformable to the image of His Son."

The new life is the participation in the living reality of Christ, in His original image, His disposition, His life, and His right. He is the new man properly speaking, the ancestor of the holy generation.[69] He is the "firstborn," who came from the womb of Mary, which is the womb of grace. But we are His brethren, together with Him, children of one Father and co-heirs of His heritage. Those whom God has so foreknown and predestined, He has called, justified, and brought to glory. Step by step, the sacred event moves toward its consummation.

∽

What shall we then say to these things?
If God is for us, who is against us?
He who spared not even His own Son
but delivered Him up for us all,
will He not also give us all things with Him?
Who shall accuse the elect of God?
God who justifieth.
Who is he who shall condemn?
Christ Jesus who died, who is risen again,
who is at the right hand of God,
who also maketh intercession for us.
Who, then, shall separate us from the love of Christ?
Shall tribulation, or distress, or famine, or nakedness,

[69] Rom. 5:12-21.

or danger, or persecution, or the sword?
But in all these things, we overcome,
because of Him who hath loved us.
For I am sure that neither death, nor life,
nor angels, nor principalities, nor powers,
nor things present, nor things to come,
nor might, nor height, nor depth,
nor any other creature shall be able
to separate us from the love of God,
which is in Christ Jesus our Lord.[70]

And now there appears to be a leap in the thought. The feeling changes. After the great confidence, one perceives a mood of uncertainty. Something seems to take place within the speaker. In his heart, which was so filled with the consciousness of his own insufficiency, in which there burned the unquenchable pain that finds expression in so many passages of his letters — because he did not deserve to be called an apostle, because he had persecuted the Church of God — there must have arisen the troubled thought: "Is this really true? Are there not too many charges against me? Cannot the 'accuser of mankind' rise up against me and say that I am not worthy of the promise?" To combat this fear, St. Paul casts himself the more passionately and unconditionally into the mystery of the love of God.

The first sentence expresses his hesitation: "What, then, shall we say?" We feel the uncertainty beneath the words, and then the complete casting of himself upon God. We recall

[70] Cf. Rom. 8:31-35, 37-39.

similar words in the New Testament: for instance, those of the man who had begged Jesus to heal his afflicted son, and when asked, "Do you believe that I can do this?" replied, "I believe; help my unbelief."[71] Recall the words spoken by Peter when, in Capernaum, after the proclamation of the mystery of the Eucharist, men were falling away on all sides, the Jews leaving first, then many disciples. Finally, as Jesus turned to the Twelve and said, "Will you also go away?" Peter, surmounting the troubled thoughts that rose within him, cast himself into the arms of the Lord: "To whom shall we go? Thou hast the words of eternal life."[72] There are moments when faith may no longer investigate and argue. Everything is at stake, and only one thing is possible: to risk all. This is the case here.

"If God is for us, then who is against us?" "Is this true? Has His grace pardoned the wrong that I have committed, so that the adversary can no longer reproach me with it? Can grace so completely overcome the evil in me that it no longer rises against God?" And it is not merely clear memory and definite knowledge that asks this question, but the oppressive fear and melancholy that has no reason. How do I know that God is for me? It is an evil question, and woe to him who yields to it.

Therefore the speaker does not admit it and above all uncertainty sets up the great affirmation of faith: "It is so, for the Spirit tells me."

But how can I be sure that it is really the Spirit who tells me? It must be He, for when He speaks, we cannot doubt. The interior beginning bears witness to itself, and it is only

---

[71] Mark 9:23.

[72] John 6:69 (RSV = John 6:68).

necessary that man shall join himself for better or for worse, to Him who "bears witness."

From this consideration, the next sentences receive their triumphant certainty. God has given His Son for us; that means He has revealed a disposition of which the world can have no conception. From the worldly point of view, there can be no concept of a god who acts in this way. For the world, it is a scandal. We have said that the average man finds this idea disgusting. If we wish to attain truth, we must approach the thought in another way. The very fact that God has done this thing constitutes the revelation; it shows us clearly who He is — and who man is.

∞

We hear that man does not live by his own power and merit, but by the grace of God. That is a mystery, but, if we may say so, it remains within reach of our religious thought. But when we hear further that this grace means that God delivers His own Son, and that means Himself, into an inconceivable state of strangeness and self-surrender,[73] we cannot escape the conclusion that man must be something that makes such surrender worthwhile in the eyes of God; not because of man's own being and merit, but because of what God gave him when He created him.

And the gift that God gave is truly man's. When God created him, He created him as important for Himself. He created him as His own destiny in a way we cannot imagine.

[73] Cf. Phil. 2:7-8.

And the Word Dwelt Among Us

And if we take seriously the message that God loves man —
truly loves him, not just in some way and metaphorically
speaking — and if we consider that He is the one who loves,
we can perhaps guess what that may mean.

This love is so powerful and all-sufficient that no accusa-
tion can find a place. For a man of Paul's strong and sensitive
conscience, who constantly feels that his actions and his
character are being weighed, the whole of life is a single
judgment. The accuser is his conscience, and beneath his
conscience the melancholy of his temperament oppresses him,
and still deeper down is the dark fiend who observes the evil
in man. It is a dreadful thing if the defender is not strong —
strong enough to overcome fear. Otherwise fear increases, and
the darkness is victorious. But the defender is there, Christ
Jesus, who, in His whole existence, is the revelation of that
love of God — He who died and rose again and is enthroned
in glory.

But again doubt and fear may intrude and cause confusion:
Christ is there, it is true, but is He there for me? "He is," Paul's
faith replies, "for He loves me." His fear says, "Do you know
that He loves you?" Faith replies, "I know it, for His whole
existence is nothing but love." "But perhaps you have become
unworthy of this love, for you opposed Him at one time. He
Himself cried out to you that day on the way to Damascus,
'Saul, Saul, why do you persecute me?' "[74] Now the point has
been reached again when argument must cease, because every
answer provokes a new doubt, and the confusion of fear per-
meates and rises above everything. Again all is at stake, and so

[74] Acts 9:4.

faith becomes a single affirmation: "Nothing can separate us from the love of Christ"; nothing from without or from within; nothing that belongs to the world or to the powers of darkness.

These words are a single crescendo of faith triumphing over the objections that arise on all sides — a single hymn of that same consciousness that we have previously called "hope." The innermost being of man, "the heart of his heart" to use the marvelous words of the poet, unites with the innermost being of God, with His will and His nature as revealed in Christ, with His love. When this happens, when this innermost being of man clasps and clings to the love of God, then the decision has been carried out. This is the center of the world. Then anything may come — misfortune and destruction and perplexity: the essential thing is secure. Even more, even better, "All things work for good." What we have previously called the certainty of the developing new life here becomes a victory.

∞

The Canticle of Love

∞

I will show you
a more excellent way.

If I speak with the tongues
of men and of angels,
and have not love,
I am become as sounding brass,
or a tinkling cymbal.

And if I should have prophecy and
should know all mysteries and all knowledge,
and if I should have all faith,
so that I could move mountains,
and have not love,
I am nothing.

And if I should distribute
all my goods to feed the poor,
and if I should deliver
my body to be burned,
and have not love,
it profiteth me nothing.

Love is patient, is kind; love envieth not,
dealeth not perversely, is not puffed up;
is not ambitious, seeketh not its own;
is not provoked to anger, thinketh no evil;
rejoiceth not in iniquity,
but rejoiceth with the truth;
beareth all things, believeth all things,
hopeth all things, endureth all things.

Love never falleth away:
whether prophecies shall be made void,
or tongues shall cease, or knowledge shall be destroyed.
For we know in part, and we prophesy in part,
but when that which is perfect is come,
that which is in part shall be put away.

When I was a child, I spoke as a child,
I understood as a child, I thought as a child.
But when I became a man,
I put away the things of a child.

We see now through a glass in a dark manner;
but then face-to-face.
Now I know in part; but then I shall know
even as I am known.

And now there remain faith, hope, and love,
these three: but the greatest of these is love.

1 Corinthians 12:31, 13:1-13

✂

In the Sacred Scriptures, there are
some texts which are particularly precious. There is something of perfection and completeness about them — like a poem. So we read them again and again, discuss them and refer to them. This is a good thing. Such texts form, as it were, points of agreement in the Christian spiritual life. But by the same token, they may suffer harm; they may become trite, slip into the commonplace, and take on a deficient or incorrect meaning.

In dealing with such texts, the interpreter's task is above all to restore to them their greatness and their mystery. The superficiality of daily use makes it seem as if the word of God has become familiar and has been penetrated and exhausted. It appears "old," that is, dissolved, in the composite of the world, in the context of human thought. But the word of the revelation is of its nature "new," because it comes from beyond the world and can never be absorbed by it.

Essentially, one generation does not know more than the preceding one merely because men have thought thirty years longer about a word of Scripture. For every generation, for every person, for every hour, God's word exists only in the form of a revelation. And this means that nothing which precedes can make it easier to understand, but that it must be understood at all times and by all men according to the inmost predisposition of faith.

To produce this newness is the first and foremost task of interpretation.

A text that particularly requires such a restoration to its newness is the thirteenth chapter of the first letter to the Corinthians. It has been called the Canticle of Love, has been treated from the most widely different points of view, referred to on all imaginable occasions, and so it has suffered a sad fate. It has been taken ethically, and in that way, it has lost all its living quality. It has been taken emotionally, and so it has become sentimental and frivolous. It has been compared with other texts that deal with love, especially with Plato, and in this way, it has been brought so close to the latter that Plato became half-Christian and Paul half-pagan; or else, men have taken the Greek philosopher as a measure and proved how scant and poor were the Christian apostle's ideas of love.

Therefore we must ask what the text really means. And the first approach depends on a very simple fact — namely, that this thirteenth chapter stands between the twelfth and the fourteenth. That sounds foolish, for where else should it stand? But this aspect of the situation appears to be rarely noticed. The chapter is not as much of a unit as it is usually regarded, but it is integrally connected with the other two and receives its meaning only from them. For they deal with the early Christian spiritual gifts (*charismata*),[75] and it is in reference to these that the nature of love is defined.

[75] 1 Cor. 12:8-11.

∽

When the Son of God came to us, the event took place in the silent manner of birth. The coming of the Spirit occurred in a different way — as an irruption and a shock. Like a mighty wind, He came to us from the remoteness of God. The house was filled with the sound. Flames leaped up. Men were gripped, shaken, overwhelmed. And the power of the event was made manifest in another peculiar way. The book of Acts relates, "And all were filled with the Holy Spirit and began to speak in other tongues, as the Spirit gave them to speak, so that pilgrims who had come to Jerusalem from various countries said in amazement, 'We hear them speak in our tongues the great deeds of God.' "[76]

If we consider this in connection with other passages, the phenomenon could be explained in this way: The disciples are gripped by the power of the Spirit; they experience an interior transformation; the fullness of the reality of Christ becomes clear to them; the glory of Christ overwhelms them. They are beside themselves, and the tremendous experience overflows in broken words and exclamations, perhaps even in mere stammering. Those of the hearers who are prepared and open their hearts to what is taking place are so far gripped by the same power of the Spirit that they enter into harmony with the speakers and their ears comprehend what is meant; but those who shut their hearts and resist hear only a senseless stammering. They mock and say, "These men are filled with new wine."[77]

[76] Acts 2:4, 11.
[77] Acts 2:13.

The breaking forth of the Spirit is not confined to that hour. When the storm breaks, new blasts constantly succeed each other. The book of Acts recounts that the first Christian congregations were wholly filled with this experience. Whenever an unusual event took place — for instance, if a great danger was averted or men came to the Faith in a significant way — or when the Apostles laid their hands upon new converts, "the Spirit came upon them"[78] and filled them with His power. In the life of the early congregations, the most varied effects of the Spirit's work were manifest. Sometimes these were so strong that the essential thing — namely, the quiet response that faith and daily life give to the word of revelation — suffered eclipse in the consciousness of the faithful.

A number of such gifts of the Spirit are named. The most conspicuous was the speaking in tongues, mentioned above. Then there was prophecy, when a believer was so powerfully gripped by one of the saving truths that he proclaimed it in a powerful, overwhelming manner. Then there was the gift of discernment, which revealed the condition of another's soul; the gift of wisdom, which understood the hidden meaning of things; and the gift of faith, when faith acquired a kind of power and healed the sick or performed other miracles.

These workings of the Spirit made the religious life of the early congregations very strong. They clearly defined the difference that existed between the old and the new, assured the believer, convinced the stranger, and acted as sparks that spread a conflagration. At the same time, they contained the danger inherent in all that is extraordinary: that motives of an

[78] Acts 19:6.

evil nature, such as vanity, ambition, jealousy, and envy, would mingle with them; that the Christian attitude would slip into the superficially enthusiastic, the frenzied, one might almost say the Dionysiac; that reality and its order, the faith and action of everyday life, might withdraw and everything might somehow become fantastic and visionary. And as a matter of fact, this danger frequently materialized, and the Apostles had to resist it. In any case, we know that this was true of St. Paul in relation to the congregation in Corinth.

Corinth was known to be very cultured, very unreliable, pleasure-seeking, and eager for new sensations. When a man becomes a Christian, he is converted, but he is not magically transformed. His heart is touched by the message and his will resolves to obey, but in disposition and natural character, he remains the man he was. So the congregation of Corinth surely had the good will of a Christian community. It even possessed — and this was the mark of a true religious emotion — the plenitude of the gifts of the Spirit. The letter of the apostle proves that.

But the people, even as Christians, were Corinthians. So we read, for example, that there were among them very serious moral difficulties, and that the Corinthians were critical of the apostle and inclined to deride him. Hence there were various unsavory motives connected with the gifts of the Spirit in their case. There seems to have developed a kind of virtuosity of religious peculiarity and, with it, manifestations of jealousy and envy in a field in which they are most inappropriate. The Greek tendency toward religious frenzy, toward absorption in the impersonal Dionysiac element also appears to have made itself felt.

In consequence, a strange situation developed: strong charismatic experiences, of which it was not certain whether they
were really Christian and did not glide off in other directions;
highly developed religious endowments which, however, did
not concern themselves with the simplest exigencies of the
life of the congregation and which failed in daily duties.

All this St. Paul attacks in the twelfth and fourteenth
chapters of the letter of which we are speaking, and the
thirteenth stands between them and forms the core of his
whole train of thought.

∞

Now, concerning spiritual things, my brethren,
I would not have you ignorant.
You know that when you were heathens,
you went to dumb idols, according as you were led.
Wherefore I give you to understand that no man,
speaking by the Spirit of God, saith, "Jesus be cursed."
And no man can say, "the Lord Jesus,"
but by the Holy Spirit.[79]

These sentences reveal the whole danger. The congregation was full of religious powers and experiences. But the
apostle saw that these were uncertain things and gave the
Corinthians what is so important in religious life, a standard
by which to distinguish. He says: religious experiences — those
you have known previously in religious festivals and mysteries — are not the essential thing. Mere religious experience is

[79] 1 Cor. 12:1-3.

ambiguous; it receives its character only in our decision before the word and will of God, and that means before Christ. A religious manifestation may be as mighty, as glowing, as convincing as possible, but if it turns against Christ in any way, it is not of God. But if a religious manifestation culminates in the confession of Christ, in the cry, "You, O Christ, are the Lord, the risen Savior," it can come only from God.

These words fall like an illuminating and dividing ray into a religious chaos.

The next verses give us the most exhaustive description of the early Christian *charismata* that the New Testament contains.[80] But before the enumeration, as well as after it, St. Paul emphasizes that "there are diversities of gifts," but that "it is one Spirit who works in all and gives to each the particular gift that He will."[81] The argument is obviously directed against those who use the graces of the Spirit for purposes of vanity and jealousy.

Thereupon follows the fine passage in which St. Paul evaluates the graces from the point of view of his teaching on the Mystical Body.[82] The believers are not only individuals externally related to each other, but form a living unity, the Church. A single common life envelops them; in this, each one forms a member, a cell, as we would say today. As every cell has its special function and, in that very way, serves the whole, so does each believer in the totality of the Christian life.

[80] 1 Cor. 12:4-11.
[81] Cf. 1 Cor. 12:4, 11.
[82] 1 Cor. 12:12-30.

The Spirit is the life-principle of the Church, but also of each individual. He gives to each his particular life in relation to the whole. The *charismata* are expressions of this, entrusted to the recipient not for his private existence, but for the whole, and he perverts their meaning if he becomes conceited about them or envies others or disparages one gift in comparison with another. And even if one gift should be inferior, that would merely be a reason to treat it with greater consideration. The peculiar phenomenon of the *charismata* in this way is set in an order — namely, the totality of the Christian community; the individual recipient of the graces is instructed to treat his fellow Christian with respect and kindliness.

The fourteenth chapter again takes up the question of the *charismata*, at least from the point of view of Christian community life. But the image which illustrates it is not that of the body and its members, but of the assembled congregation. St. Paul represents to his audience the faithful individually practicing their charismatic powers.

Who will be more useful to the congregation: he who speaks with tongues or he who is prophetically enlightened? The former is not understood by the others, unless they themselves are seized by the same Spirit. In him, only his inner self speaks, his spirit; his understanding does nothing.[83] The rapture remains in his immediate experience and does not pass over into thought and word. The result is that the bystander cannot "speak his *Amen* to the other's praise";[84] no communion is established.

[83] 1 Cor. 14:14.
[84] Cf. 1 Cor. 14:16.

But the gift of prophecy is concerned with the word and requires thought. So the one who is prophetically gifted is able to announce truth and reveal the secrets of hearts. The effect is that the person concerned "falls upon his face and adores God."[85] But when those who are inspired by the prophetic spirit speak, it should not be done in a disorderly way, so that many speak at the same time, "for God is not a God of confusion but of peace."[86] They should "prophesy in proper order, so that all may learn and be admonished."[87] But if a word is incomprehensible, they should see to it that "one may interpret."[88]

From all this he draws the conclusion: "Do not hinder the speaking with tongues," but "seek after the gift of prophecy"; as for the rest, "let all things be done decently and in order."[89] The spiritual gifts are good in themselves, for the Spirit bestows them, so they should have a free field. But they should be fitted into the life of the community and promote this life. Their respective value is to be measured not according to the regard which they may bring to the individual, but according to their usefulness to the community. The more clear, helpful, and fruitful, the better they are. At the same time, it becomes evident that whereas the gift comes from the Spirit, the man has a certain influence, in that he asks for one rather than another, or perhaps checks or promotes their interior

---

[85] Cf. 1 Cor. 14:25.

[86] 1 Cor. 14:33.

[87] 1 Cor. 14:31.

[88] 1 Cor. 14:27.

[89] 1 Cor. 14:39-40.

And the Word Dwelt Among Us

development. So St. Paul says, "Be zealous for the better gifts";[90] and again, "Be zealous for spiritual gifts, but rather that you may prophesy."[91]

∞

With these two sentences, the twelfth chapter ends and the fourteenth begins. Between them stands the thirteenth chapter, on love.

Its meaning becomes clear if we adduce the second half of the preceding verse: "But I will show you a more excellent way."[92] And then follow the words: "If I speak with the tongues of men and of angels, and have not love, I am become as sounding brass, or a tinkling cymbal. And if I should have prophecy and should know all mysteries and all knowledge, and if I should have all faith, so that I could move mountains, and have not love, I am nothing. And if I should distribute all my goods to feed the poor, and if I should deliver my body to be burned, and have not love, it profiteth me nothing."[93]

Here several of the spiritual gifts are taken up again, and their significance and insignificance are demonstrated from one point of view, which was prepared for in the preceding chapter and is concluded in the following one — namely, love.

A person may have the gift of tongues; indeed — and now the thought leaps in Pauline fullness beyond its starting

[90] 1 Cor. 12:31.
[91] 1 Cor. 14:1.
[92] 1 Cor. 12:31.
[93] 1 Cor. 13:1-3.

point — he may have the gift of speaking in the tongues of all men, even of the higher beings, of angels, but if he has no love, then it is all empty noise. Only love gives meaning to speech; without love, it is empty. A man may have the gift of prophecy, may recognize hidden relations, behold the secret meaning of things, and be able to reveal the innermost recesses of the human heart. Without love, it is all nothing. A man may have the gift of knowledge; that probably means a deep insight into sacred truth proceeding from his inner experience. Without love, it is nothing. A man may have the *charisma* of faith, which evidently means that his faith becomes a spiritual power capable of miracles. This, too, is nothing without love. A man may have, through the working of the Spirit, an enthusiasm for self-sacrifice, so that he sacrifices himself for his neighbor and gives away everything for his sake; or for God, so that he casts himself with fiery enthusiasm into martyrdom as the Maccabees[94] did of old. Even that is nothing if it is done without love.

These sentences are very important. They tell us that there are magnificent, heroic, seemingly quite unselfish actions whose significance before God is very ambiguous. They can be forms of folly or selfishness, and therefore "nothing" by the proper standard — when they do not proceed from love. Only when they do so proceed are they "something" and of value before God. There are even actions of indubitably religious nature, experiences which, like prophecy, religious knowledge, and faith that has become a power, seem to certify

---

[94] The celebrated Jewish family whose history is recorded in the two books of Maccabees in the Old Testament. See 2 Macc. 7.

their own piety and validity, and yet are ambiguous. Even these can be nothing, an idle game of self-expression and self-indulgence, if they do not proceed from love. Only from love do both ethical greatness and religious power receive their significance before God.

Here we find repeated, from a particular point of view, what was said at the beginning of the twelfth chapter. Spiritual values, such as strength of soul, emotion of the heart, religious experience and power, need not of themselves be good. They share in the ambiguity of the world, and their ultimate quality depends on love alone. Its presence or absence gives to everything its final character. So we eagerly wait to learn how the nature of love will be defined.

∞

Love is patient, is kind;
love envieth not, dealeth not perversely,
is not puffed up; is not ambitious,
seeketh not its own;
is not provoked to anger, thinketh no evil;
rejoiceth not in iniquity,
but rejoiceth with the truth;
beareth all things, believeth all things,
hopeth all things, endureth all things.[95]

We must admit that we are surprised, even a little disappointed. Should love, which has been spoken of so emphatically, and which has been recognized as the power that gives

[95] 1 Cor. 13:4-7.

its meaning to everything, be no more than that? All that is here said about love — that it is patient, kind, without envy or vanity, not overbearing, but well-behaved, unselfish, self-controlled, ready to forgive, not rejoicing in evil, but ready to rejoice in the good — are these not just everyday virtues? But when we consider the matter more closely, we see that it is just this that contains the meaning of the whole argument. The *charismata* are manifestations of a religious peculiarity which is perhaps connected with natural talents, with geniality or heroism. Love is contrasted with this as being the essential thing, love in the form of simple truth, goodness, and faithfulness of life.

The unusual phenomenon can belong to the realm of mere experience, of imagination, even of vanity, and, on that very account, can be "nothing," empty in itself and without power to master reality. With this, love is contrasted, love in a form that has nothing of superficial religious experience, glow, or original talent, but which is "something": reality — reality in itself, because it is pure in value and genuine in action, and really powerful in the world, because it is capable of mastering life as it is.

Love is actually portrayed as Christian sobriety, but a sobriety which has nothing to do with barrenness of heart or narrowness of mind. If it gives significance to the *charismata*, it must come from the heart of God, from the operation of the Holy Spirit. It must be moderation in fullness, the "sober intoxication of the Spirit," as the old hymn says, an attitude which, in its serene self-control, its faithfulness and strength, is incomparably greater, deeper, and richer than all that is unusual.

In the final sentence, the power and universality that were veiled by the other statements break forth. Love "bears all things." Elsewhere St. Paul says, "Each shall bear the other's burden,"[96] his need, his weakness, his importunities. Love "believes all things." Since this refers to faith in regard to other men, we might perhaps rather say that it believes them capable of all good, encourages with faith and confidence the living potentialities in others. It "hopes all things," desires all good things for others and expects all that is fine from them. It "endures all things," all pain that comes from others.

∞

Love never falleth away: whether prophecies
shall be made void, or tongues shall cease
or knowledge shall be destroyed.
For we know in part, and we prophesy in part,
but when that which is perfect is come,
that which is in part shall be put away.
When I was a child, I spoke as a child, I understood
as a child, I thought as a child. But when I
became a man, I put away the things of a child.
We see now through a glass in a dark manner;
but then face-to-face.
Now I know in part; but then
I shall know even as I am known.
And now there remain faith, hope, and love,
these three: but the greatest of these is love.[97]

[96] Cf. Gal. 6:2.
[97] 1 Cor. 13:8-13.

The first section of the chapter stated that the spiritual gifts, which were so overrated by the recipients of the letter, receive their meaning not from themselves, but from love. This is the essential core. The second section considered the nature of love as consisting in honesty and the simple realities of daily action, again in contrast to the extraordinary nature of the spiritual gifts. In the third section, love is again contrasted with the gifts, this time as that which abides; whereas they pass away, love does not pass away.

The spiritual gifts belong to our transitory earthly existence. Prophecy has a meaning as long as our life is carried on within the bounds of time and place, of secret inwardness. Here it is very important if the prophet has the gift to proclaim what shall one day take place, to tell those present in a certain place what is happening at a distance, to reveal in his true nature the man who conceals his real opinions from others and perhaps even from himself. But all this is in relation to sacred history, which takes place in time, for the prophet beholds the secret operations by which God ordains events, and interprets therefrom what takes place at any one time. But these accomplishments lose their significance when the end of all things, of the world and of the life of the individual, makes everything eternally manifest.

Speaking with tongues is also bound up with the limitations of earthly existence, with the inadequacy of speech. Man does not know God. Between him and the living Lord lies the dullness of his earthly nature. His earthliness separates him from the mysterious and remote Divinity. His sin makes him blind to the One who is all-holy. Hence his experience of God remains inadequate, uncertain, and ambiguous. But when the

Spirit visits a man, he comes face-to-face with God in immediate experience, and knows who He is. But he cannot express
it. In speaking with tongues, he vainly attempts to break the
barrier. "It is speech, but spoken in the air,"[98] because no one
understands it. It is a "prayer," a communion with God, in
which "my spirit prays, but my mind can do nothing."[99] Everything remains in the inexpressibility of immediate contact and
does not succeed in finding words. With our earthly existence,
this gift also loses its significance.

The charismatic knowledge will also disappear. Man is
driven by the desire for truth — but it is a truth which does
not consist merely in grasping facts, in beholding the nature
of things and understanding their logical connection. He
would like to know what is before him, why it is so and where
it leads, how it comes from the whole, and what it is in itself.
He would like to understand the fact from the essence and the
temporal from the eternal. He would like to grasp the ultimate
which leaves no further question, but reveals all things in the
openness of truth. But he cannot do this, because, in this
respect also, his existence is limited.

The gift of wisdom must have had something of this quality, but only in such a way that the spirit touched it and then
lost it again. When the hour had passed, the man could only
say, "I had it, but now it is gone." With the end of our earthly
life, everything comes into the clear present. Then the nature
of things is revealed in their appearance, the meaning is evident in every portion of being; fact and necessity correspond

[98] 1 Cor. 14:9.
[99] 1 Cor. 14:14.

to each other. Truth has become a condition, and the *charisma* no longer means anything.

And now the thought of the apostle proceeds from the *charismata* of knowledge or understanding to understanding in general. Spiritual understanding is a partial thing; prophecy is a partial thing — all our understanding is partial. It belongs to our earthly existence, just as a child's way of understanding belongs to his age. The child has his way of speaking, of feeling, of thinking; as soon as he is grown, all this ceases, and his ways become those of a man. Man upon earth is but a child. He never reaches that ripeness of truth which consists in seeing the whole and the individual thing in their relation, and both clearly and openly. He always sees only parts, pieces, and he sees them dimly, hidden in himself, because he sees the essential not immediately but in reflection. Things do not exist in themselves, but are rooted in another, the essential and eternal. In order to understand them correctly, we must grasp them in their essential and eternal root, but this never appears to our eyes. It is as if a man could not view immediately the thing with which he is concerned, but only in a mirror, and a mirror which is dark and uneven, so that the figure appears wavering and broken.

Someday it will be different. We shall see "face-to-face." The phrase is so common that we do not notice at once what a great fact it expresses — namely, that the essential, which alone is ultimately worth knowing and in which all else finds its truth, is a "face." It is God, He whom we everywhere behold in dark, indistinct mirrors, which conceal rather than reveal. One day He will look at us openly, and the veil shall be taken away from our own face, so that it can freely turn to Him. And in everything, the face of God will shine forth, and from this face, each thing will receive its truth — that truth which consists in being the content of His eternal knowledge, and which makes it possible for us to discover and know anything. All our knowledge is contained within the knowledge of God.

The little sentence contains even more; this is shown by what follows. The "face" with which man shall behold the face of God is not his completed possession. It is not as if he must look into the mirror here on earth and then simply turn around and behold the sacred countenance. Considered as a face or an eye, man is just as dark, confused, and interiorly broken as the mirror of things. But if on earth he has had faith in the self-revealing God and has persevered in the dimness of his earthly existence, he will be given that face which can turn to God, and with those eyes, he shall know as he is known.

The foundation of all truth is the knowledge of God. The beginning of all knowledge lies in Him. God's knowledge is the presupposition for the thing's being knowable and makes it possible for men to know it. The fact that God knows all things, that every being is from its very root known by God, is now hidden. We say it over to ourselves, try to realize it, but do not experience it. Things stand before us as unrevealed riddles, dark lumps of being. Knowledge seems to begin only when man faces them; they themselves in their own being seem to have nothing to do with this. The world could exist even if no one knew it, just as the silent wastes of ice around the poles exist even if no eye beholds them.

But one day it will become clear that before the being of things comes their being known; that they were never un-known, because otherwise they could never have existed. The being of things is a fruit of God's knowledge. And that they shall dawn upon us in their reality and essentiality is possible only because they stand wholly in the knowledge of God. Everything exists in consequence of the knowledge of God, but we do not perceive this.

Herein lies the hiddenness of existence, the illusion that the world is a beginning and exists in itself, a beginning of mere existence, followed only later, perhaps after endless effort and slow progress, by its being known by man. This illusion is a part and parcel of sin. One day it shall fall away, and it shall be revealed that the world exists only in consequence of its being known by God — the world and we ourselves also. I shall realize that I exist only because God knows me. My being known by God is my reality, and I become real in the measure that my life and action are in harmony with the knowledge of God. And my knowledge is true in the measure in which it agrees with the divine knowledge. Now we understand the immensity of the sentence: One day I shall know completely, "even as I am known." I shall share in the glance which God casts upon me, and shall return this glance to God. From the knowledge of God, I shall know His holy countenance, and therein all things.

This will be eternity, the essential and unending. All else shall pass away, even the spiritual gifts which seem so powerful, so glowing, and so great to him who receives them — to him and also to the one who envies him. One day there shall be nothing but pure brightness, quiet genuineness, the perfectly fulfilled presence of this "face-to-face."

The final sentence has a blended meaning. "Now there abide faith, hope, and love, these three; but the greatest of these is love." We do not see at once what the words "now there abide" mean. St. Paul thinks passionately. His thought ferments and overflows, so that the same word at times has one meaning and suggests another. Primarily *abide* signifies the contrast to the transitoriness of existence. Everything earthly passes away, even the *charismata*. But faith, hope, and love are forces that extend into eternity. They are gifts of the Holy Spirit, like the others, but not given merely to help within the boundaries of time and to disappear with time: they are an already-beginning eternity, which shall one day be perfected.

But then another thought slips in: even faith and hope are bound up with time. The letter to the Romans says, "We are saved by hope. But hope whose object is seen is not hope. If it is seen, why should we still hope? But if our hope is directed toward that which we do not yet see, then let us wait in patience."[100] The same God who gives the *charismata* is He who produces the power of this hope, namely, patience. But one day that will no longer be needed. Faith, too, shall disappear in an existence in which we see face-to-face, and so shall the mirror and its riddle.

And so, from the trinity of those gifts which, in contrast with the *charismata*, prove abiding, St. Paul finally selects one as the greatest: love. Its greatness consists in the fact that it never passes away, as he said at the beginning of the passage, but is, in the final sense of the word, abiding.

Now it becomes clear what the ultimate criterion is by which St. Paul measures the manifestations of the Christian life. It is their power to resist transitoriness; it is their closeness

[100]Rom. 8:24-25.

to eternity. The *charismata* are quite transitory. They belong to time and its limitations. If he had been questioned on the subject, St. Paul would have admitted that they were not even essential for the progress of historical Christianity as a whole, but were bound up with a definite period. They are expressions of an eruption and its exuberance — phenomena of the youthful Christianity which disappear as soon as mature age with its severity and commonplace begins. This spiritual condition can recur in times of historical crisis, but in as fleeting a manner as in the beginning.

By contrast, faith and hope have an essential character. A man can be a Christian without the *charismata*, but not without faith and hope. These have an eternal content even now. Eternal life is already present. Death and God's merciful judgment do not bestow it, but set it free and perfect it. Eternity is not a space into which man shall one day step, but it is the character which the redeemed life within him possesses from the beginning. It is the manner in which God lives and the manner in which man, through the grace of God, shares in the life of God.

At present, it is enclosed in the transitory, and we perceive it only through the interior assurance in which, as the letter to the Romans says, "the Holy Spirit bears witness with our spirit that we are children of God."[101] But one day it shall come forth, open its eyes, and become self-conscious and joyful. Then faith and hope shall pass away. But not love. It shall only then awaken to the fullness of its power and its freedom. It shall be the very act of our eternal life.

[101]Rom. 8:16.

This is the last thing that St. Paul says about it here, and by which he contrasts it with all else: love is eternal.

∽

But let us not permit this word to be used carelessly as has happened to so many of the sacred words. The meaning of the word *eternal* has nothing to do with its use in popular language. Its real meaning is not made clear in the thirteenth chapter of the first letter to the Corinthians. If we look closely, we see that the question — what love in itself is — is not asked here, but only how love conducts itself and how it lasts. What is it, then?

In order to answer this question, we must refer to other texts. If we consider only the chapter of first Corinthians which contrasts love with the overrated and misused spiritual gifts, love appears as something ethical, even with a certain inclination to the bourgeois, as moderation and consideration. But this does not completely express the thought of the apostle. He holds that the love which is demanded of man does not originate in man himself, but in God. Of the love of God we read in other letters: for instance, in the one to the Romans. In the passage where St. Paul, as it were, casts his anchor in the love of God as the center of Christian life, we read, "What shall we then say to these things? If God is for us, who is against us? He who spared not even His own Son, but delivered Him up for us all, will He not also give us all things with Him? Who shall accuse the elect of God? God who justifieth. Who is he who shall condemn? Christ Jesus who died, who is risen again, who is at the right hand of God, who also maketh intercession for us. Who, then, shall separate us from the love of Christ? Shall tribulation, or distress, or famine, or naked-ness, or danger, or persecution, or the sword? But in all these things, we overcome, because of Him who hath loved us. For I am sure that neither death, nor life, nor angels, nor princi-palities, nor powers, nor things present, nor things to come, nor might, nor height, nor depth, nor any other creature shall be able to separate us from the love of God, which is in Christ Jesus our Lord."[102]

Here in Romans, that power breaks through which is lack-ing in our text from first Corinthians. But we must mentally supply it behind every sentence of this chapter of first Corin-thians, so that it fills and animates its self-controlled sobriety. The love of which St. Paul is speaking is not the force of human passion or affection or kindliness which the word expresses in popular parlance, but it is a power and disposition of God. And we must not, as generally happens, think of it after the manner of our own love (only very pure and great), but we must, in speaking of the love of God, first of all, forget what the word means in our language and remember that we are here concerned with Revelation. We must listen to its words and receive its meaning purely from its own expression.

That God loves may be self-evident, as an expression of perfect and complete existence; that He loves man is by no means self-evident. Natural religious experience does not per-ceive the divine merely in the form of goodness and kindness; witness the gods of hatred and horror of which we hear in the history of religion, the references to the indifference, the envy,

[102]Rom. 8:31-35, 37-39.

the anger of the gods, to the incomprehensibility of the dispensations of fate, and other such things. Even the experiences of divine goodness do not mean at all what the New
Testament means by *love*, but merely indicate that the divine
ruler is gracious, takes pleasure in His creatures, is rich and
inclined to share His riches. But the New Testament reveals
to us in the love of God a seriousness which, if we remove the
dulling effect of custom that lies upon all Christian concepts,
must affect us more and more deeply.

This love is not something which God, as would be in
accord with our ideas, hands down to His creature, man; not a
radiation of His favor which does not affect Him; but it is
something unheard of, which we can express only if we speak
quite recklessly. The fact that God has created a world and
men in this world would not in itself need to touch Him in His
own existence. It would simply be a creation, separated absolutely from Him, the Creator, by the very fact of its having
been created. He would take pleasure in it, behold its perfec-
tions, the work of His creation, desire its welfare and its
consummation, and guide it to that end by His governing
Providence. But, for all that, it would not need to touch His
heart in any way. He would not have to be interiorly concerned with it.

What the Greeks said about the Olympian repose of their
gods who sit enthroned above all earthly turmoil hints at this
idea. This is as far as the concept of divine love which we could
reach by ourselves would go, unless we went to the other
extreme and conceived it in Dionysiac fashion, as a kind of
universal intoxication of the divinity, as it appears in the case
of a number of gods in the history of religion. But that this has

nothing to do with the chaste God of Revelation goes without saying.

What Revelation says about the love of God breaks down, as it were, the barrier that His divinity erects between Him and the world. It tells us that the world means something to Him — far beyond all that we could deduce from our ideas of God and His creation. He is Lord of the world in inviolable freedom, but He has given it a meaning for Himself, has drawn it close to Him, and in a kind of closeness which we can express only by saying that He has let it become His destiny. If we wish to conceive of this, we must be on our guard that we do not violate the absolute lordship of God or veil the inexorable createdness of the world. This is the first and fundamental truth about the love of God.

But it is equally true that He has drawn the world into the depth of His own existence in a way that establishes between God and us a relation which, from a human point of view, is incomprehensible and impossible. This forms the essential content of the Christian message and is "the love of God."[103]

What else can it mean if St. Paul says that God "did not spare His own Son, but delivered Him up for us all"? And immediately thereafter: "Christ it is who died for us, and who also rose again and sits at the right hand of God and intercedes for us." What else can the word of St. John mean: "God so loved the world that He gave His only-begotten Son"?[104]

Let us not take such sentences as self-evident. If God wished to receive us back into His favor after we had fallen

---

[103]Rom. 8:39.
[104]John 3:16.

away from Him, He could have done so without involving Himself. He is God; an act of indulgence or of newly creating forgiveness would have been sufficient, and that would have been mysterious enough. It would be presumptuous and foolish as well to try to maintain that a greater price was necessary for the redemption of man.

But now we hear that God "gave His Son," that is, Himself. Gave for what? And to whom? This is the decisive thing. He let Himself be seized by something from which He was exempt by virtue of His divinity — namely, destiny.

But what could deliver Him up to this destiny, which of itself had no power over Him? What can "destiny" be for God? Only a power which would rise up in Himself, in His own inviolable freedom — a power of honor and of love. Let us leave the former aside; it would bring up the whole problem of God, as the great Doctor of the Church, St. Anselm of Canterbury,[105] did.

Let us stay with the second point: the love of God. It is that incomprehensible will with which He permitted the creature to approach Him in such a way that He "must" now solve the problem of its destiny, not through an aloof and omnipotent Providence, but through the "giving" of Himself; by entering into history, living among us, and rising victorious over death and sin. This is the work of that love of which the New Testament speaks.

And now St. Paul says this love is still in operation as that disposition with which Christ stands before God for our sake. It is the one and all, the beginning and the end for us. Our new

---

[105]St. Anselm (c. 1033-1109), Archbishop of Canterbury.

existence is rooted and grounded in it, as the reality of creation is grounded in the almighty will of Him who created it.

This love by which we live as Christians should also be the disposition and the strength in which we deal with other men. From it there shall grow a new life-relation, a new order of things. This is presupposed by all that has been said about Christian love. If St. Paul opposes the sobriety of Christian love to the enthusiasm of the *charismata*, it is not in order to draw it into the ethical or sentimental or earthly, but to contrast it as the truly real and lasting thing with phenomena that very easily slip into the fantastic, and, in any case, are transitory.

But he would say of this same love that it is immensity itself, so far surpassing all our concepts that it can be known only through Revelation and must constantly be grasped and held by means of this. The sublimity of the thought processes underlying St. Paul's doctrine of love is shown by the twelfth chapter of the letter to the Corinthians, in which the relation of the individual believers to each other is indicated by the figure of the mystical Christ.

But if we wish to hear how the simple teachings of the thirteenth chapter would sound if St. Paul uttered them from their real depths, then we must look at the letter to his favorite congregation, the Philippians. Here we find sentences like this: "God is my witness how I long for you all in the heart of Jesus Christ."[106] It is the loving intimacy of Christ Himself with which he loves. That core of love, of which he says in the letter to the Romans that no power of the world "can separate

[106]Phil. 1:8.

us from the love of God, which is in Christ our Lord," here becomes active. Only from this point of view do the simple sentences of the letter to the Corinthians receive their true magnitude. Now they are an expression of that holy moderation of Christianity with which it expresses matters for which no word would really be sufficiently fervent.

∞

Romano Guardini
(1885-1968)

Although he was born in Verona,
Italy, Romano Guardini grew up in Mainz, Germany, where his father was serving as Italian consul. Since his education and formation were German, he decided to remain in Germany as an adult.

After he had studied chemistry and economics as a youth, Guardini turned to theology and was ordained to the priesthood in 1910. From 1923 to 1939 (when he was expelled by the Nazis), Father Guardini occupied a chair especially created for him at the University of Berlin as "professor for philosophy of religion and Catholic *Weltanschauung*." After the war, similar positions were created for him — first at the University of Tübingen and then at the University of Munich (1948-1963).

Father Guardini's extremely popular courses in these universities won him a reputation as one of the most remarkable and successful Catholic educators in Germany. As a teacher, writer, and speaker, he was notable for being able to detect and nurture those elements of spirituality that nourish all that is best in the life of Catholics.

After the war, Father Guardini's influence grew to be enormous, not only through his university positions, but also through the inspiration and guidance he gave to the postwar German Catholic Youth Movement, which enlivened the faith of countless young people.

Father Guardini's writings include works on meditation, education, literature, art, philosophy, and theology. Among his dozens of books, perhaps the most famous is *The Lord*, which has been continuously in print in many languages since its first publication in 1937. Even today, countless readers continue to be transformed by these books, which combine a profound thirst for God with great depth of thought and a delightful perfection of expression.

The works of Father Guardini are indispensable reading for anyone who wants to remain true to the Faith and to grow holy in our age of skepticism and corrosive doubt.

∞

Sophia Institute Press®

∞

Sophia Institute is a nonprofit

institution that seeks to restore man's knowledge of eternal truth, including man's knowledge of his own nature, his relation to other persons, and his relation to God. Sophia Institute Press® serves this end in numerous ways. It publishes translations of foreign works to make them accessible for the first time to English-speaking readers; brings back into print books that have been long out of print; and publishes new books that fulfill the ideals of Sophia Institute. These books afford readers a rich source of the enduring wisdom of mankind.

Sophia Institute Press® makes these high-quality books available to the general public by using advanced technology and by soliciting donations to subsidize its general publishing costs. Your generosity can help Sophia Institute Press® to provide the public with editions of works containing the enduring wisdom of the ages. Please send your tax-deductible contribution to the address below. Your questions, comments, and suggestions are also welcome.

For your free catalog, call:
Toll-free: 1-800-888-9344

or write:
Sophia Institute Press®
Box 5284, Manchester, NH 03108

or visit our website:
http://www.sophiainstitute.com

Sophia Institute is a tax-exempt institution as defined by the
Internal Revenue Code, Section 501(c)(3). Tax I.D. 22-2548708.